THE MARCO POLO OF ZUBER, FLORIDA

By Dr. Gilbert L. Raiford

Second Edition

Originally published by
Dr. Staci L. Parker/DBA
Parker & Parker Publishing House
parkerandparkerpublishing@gmail.com

Copyright © 2020 Dr. Gilbert L. Raiford

All rights reserved. This book may not be reproduced in whole or in part, stored in a retrieval system, or transmitted in any form or by any means electronic, mechanical, or other without written permission from the author, except by a reviewer, who may quote brief passages in a review.

ISBN: 9798700869775

PREFACE

By Janice Raiford Alder

This is the story of an extraordinarily unique individual – a scholar, teacher, essayist, renegade, and philosopher -who is not afraid to say "yes" to every adventure that comes his way. But, more than that, it is the story of modern-day Black America and how we got from Jim Crowism to here. Dr. Raiford is often called to represent our race when interacting with the "rich and famous". He consistently mentors underprivileged youth and is a strong advocate for social justice.

Throughout the book you will find that Dr. Raiford makes no distinction between the rich and the poor; between the young and the old; and among races, religions, and persons with different sexual preferences. You will find that he easily endears himself to everyone wherever he goes and is most likely an "unforgettable character" with all who interact with him. This is a story that needs to be told and he has the ability to tell it in a most forthright manner – with lots of humor!

Synopsis: This is the story of an African American man raised in poverty in the Jim Crow south to parents who were the first generation children of formally enslaved people. It traces his roots from the backwoods of the lime mining village of Zuber, Florida to the glamour of New York City and far beyond, including travel to 13 European countries, and the continents of Africa, Asia, and Australia.

It is a story about his encounter with the Gestapo in Communist East Germany, where he was held at gun point, as well as his VIP treatment by the government of the United Kingdom, culminating in lunch with the Queen of England! Dr. Raiford tells the story about how he dodged the surveillance of an assigned "intourist" guide in Russia and traveled unescorted in Moscow.

He tells the story of how he progressed from working in the bean fields of Florida to teaching in some of the most prestigious universities in the nation. The story tells how he successfully avoided military conscription and, for six years, taught officers (mostly white) in every branch of the military.

The book also includes an impressive list of famous people with whom he has interacted, including Supreme Court Judges, McVey (The terrorist who bombed the federal building), two United States Presidents, Mrs. Eleanor Roosevelt, and the legendary Marian Anderson.

TABLE OF CONTENTS

1: Growing Up In Zuber 1

2: Hampton Institute: My Home By The Sea 22

3: From Zuber To New York City 38

4: From Zuber To Upstate Ny And Connecticut 44

5: Life As A "Beatnik" 50

7: The Beginning Of The End Of My Vagabond Days 70

8: From Zuber To Lawrence, Kansas 81

9: From Zuber To Africa 87

10: From Zuber To Chicago 93

11: Teaching In The Military 101

12: From Zuber To Washington Dc 107

13: From The Company Quarters Of Zuber To Buckingham Palace In London 114

The Epilogue 123

DEDICATION: This book is dedicated to Mildred Faulcon Raiford, my loving wife of nearly 60 years, and to our four wonderful children. They seemed to have understood and accepted my roaming spirit and my maverick behavior. They never complained when I would invite friends from Ethiopia, Nigeria, India, Germany, The Gambia, Switzerland, St Kitts, and Martinique to be our house guests, some staying months. They also tolerated, with amazing patience, my tendency to turn our home into a social service agency, including inviting the homeless and ex-felons to share Thanksgiving and Christmas dinners with us. I could not have asked for a better family. They have nurtured me as much as I have nurtured them – perhaps even more so. And for that I am truly grateful.

THANK YOU: This book might never have come to fruition without the indispensable assistance of Mr. Jerry Burnett, a friend who, on his own volition, archived all my writings that I shared with him through the years. This made it so much easier to recall incidents – both good and bad! Thank you, Jerry.

A very hearty **THANK YOU** to Ms. Jacqueline Patton of EdVisR, LLC., whose meticulous editing made this book presentable.

1: GROWING UP IN ZUBER

Living for the Weekend: Zuber, which once was a company town, lies six miles north of Ocala, Florida on old U.S. 301. To call Zuber a town is to really stretch the definition. The company, Cumber Lime, was the source of employment for all adult males and the landlord for all of the employees, meaning that they were company houses (again stretching a definition since they were clearly shacks). Houses or shacks, it didn't much matter since the price for rent was right – free! The Company also owned a store, the forerunner of Walmart, where we bought not just our food but also cooking utensils, garden supplies, schools supplies and clothing.

I was named after my father who was a demolition expert for Cumber Line Company. His father, my grandfather, had been enslaved but he was literate. Neither my father, nor his four sisters ever reached high school, but all of them were avid readers. In fact, when I was about five years old, my father read the history of the Titanic to me. I am sure that it awakened in me a thirst for knowledge, and maybe that is why I spent 33 years as a university student.

In Zuber during the Depression everyone was poor, which meant no one was poor, considering that poverty is relative. Actually, I had no idea that we were poor until I took my first sociology course in college. We always had food, clothing and shelter and did not know or care that all of these could have been better. We were satisfied – blissfully satisfied.

In Zuber, if you were big enough to eat, you were big enough to work – and work you did. At that time Marion County was easily the produce capitol of Florida, if not the entire south. Whereas the adult men worked in the lime mines of Cumber, the women and the children were gainfully employed in the produce fields. If the child labor law officials had ever taken the time to visit Zuber, not a single parent would have avoided going to jail! However, all of us really enjoyed going into the fields. For us, it was an extension of play and of course, a chance to earn our own allowances since we were able to keep all our meager pay.

Everyone in Zuber lived for the weekend! Saturday, of course, was the big fun day – the day we managed somehow to get to Ocala. It was easy to "thumb a ride" into town. Even though the Jim Crow Laws were as strict in Florida as they were in Mississippi, white motorists, mainly from the north and using 301, seemed to vie for the opportunity to pick up black hitchhikers. (Of course, we were careful to refuse rides with single white female motorists).

Anyway, Ocala was a Mecca! As soon as we would see the sign proclaiming that "We fix anything except a broken heart," we knew we were in Ocala and we would make a beeline to West Broadway! At that time, Broadway was Broadway. We did not have the glitter of Times Square, but in every other way, we had New York beat, if you discount Harlem! The town's folk relinquished Broadway to their backwoods cousins and we flooded the city with people from Reddick, Sparr, Citra, Anthony, Martin, Kendrick, Lowell, Blitchton, Cotton Plant, Micanopy, Fairfield, and several other rural hamlets.

For us, Broadway ended when it reached Magnolia. The only time we would cross Magnolia was to go to the Courthouse or shop at Woolworth's. There was no need to go farther. Everything we needed or wanted was on or near West Broadway. There was the Roxy Theater where, for 25 cents you would see the weekly news events; one or two cartoons; a serial production where every episode ended with the hero in an impossible-to-escape death situation only to return the next weekend; and a double feature movie– we clearly got our money's worth! Anyway, the only time white people would come to West Broadway would be to join us at the Roxy, but Jim Crowism prevented us from co-mingling. The problem was solved when the orchestra section was designated "white only." That suited us just fine because the view from the balcony was superior. Joining us in the balcony would always be the six Native American families still living in Silver Springs. I often wondered how they felt about us joining the white folks in rooting for the cowboys when they were clearly exploiting – and even killing the Indians. I still feel sad that I never rooted for the Indians. It never occurred to me that we must have looked just as foolish rooting for Tarzan.

But the Roxy was just the beginning. There was the Hampton Dance Hall on Broadway and we went there straight from the movie. Everyone in Zuber could dance and everyone loved to dance. More than a dance hall, the place also served booze and minors could not go in unless accompanied by an adult. (For minors to go in at all was probably illegal but who knew or who cared). Anyway, we could buy NEHI strawberry sodas and dance. It was typical to leave the dance hall and cross the other side of Broadway to Buddy Bee's to buy a bream fish sandwich on two thick slices of white Wonder bread, with a glob of yellow mustard.

By sundown, the most timid of us began to search for a ride back to the country. Most times, we would have already staked our claim to a ride and agreed on a meeting place. The most daring of us would stay in town and head for what was called "The Western Front." That was an area where Broadway extended west of downtown and was famous for its jukes or honky-tonks. If there was to be any shooting or cutting, it would take place on the Western Front. I knew of no one from our part of the backwoods who frequented the Western Front.

Sunday was our Day of Atonement – and atone we did! Sunday School started in the early morning and lasted until Church Service. *ALL* children were expected to attend Sunday School – and to remain for practically the entire day's Church service. We went home for a quick supper and returned for BYPU (Baptist Young People's Union). Traditional Baptist churches had this every Sunday evening and youth were required to attend sessions where they were expected to develop leadership skills. This time was also used for Junior Choir rehearsals. At every service, we were expected to give money and to make sure you did, the pianist would strike up the band and you had to march up front so everyone could see if you gave – and how much! In time, we learned to budget and mete out what we would give the Lord, realizing that we also had to give the devil his due!

I have traveled far beyond Zuber, but never in sentiment or fond memories.

Zuber Educational Beginnings: Our parents were the first generation of parents whose parents were slaves. They were hardworking people and great providers, but, for the most part, they were uneducated and, by extension not familiar with "proper ways to live." Therefore, refinement and social norms had to be taught, and were taught, in school. Upon reaching the age of six, every child was enrolled in Union Elementary School.

At Union there were four large classrooms. One teacher taught first and second grades; another taught third grade; and the other taught fourth. These were young African American women fresh out of college. (I stress African Americans because the original teachers were white women from northern cities who could not possibly truly understand the kind of education poor Black children needed). The fifth and sixth grades were taught by a man, who was also the principal. During my student days there, he was Mr. Alfred Hill, one of the two Zuber born and raised educators.

These early teachers really and truly understood our needs, even more than we or our parents did. In the first and second grade room, this was the routine: Everyone was expected to be in his/her assigned seat promptly at 8:00 a.m. and there was not to be a sound until the teacher greeted us with "good morning boys and girls" and, in unison, we sang back "good morning Miss Hughes." (My teacher was Miss Doris Hughes whose family was half owner of the Hughes and Chestnut Funeral Home and she drove in every day from Ocala, as did Miss McDuffy who was so short you could barely see her head over the dashboard. It was easy to think that hers was a run-a-way car with no driver)!

We had to stand and say the Pledge of Allegiance, "My Country Tis of Thee" and concluded with "Lift Every Voice and Sing". We then lined up against the wall and Miss Hughes would go from child to child to examine behind their ears and examine to see if their teeth had been brushed. She would whisper her findings to each child so as not to embarrass anyone. After that, we would sing and demonstrate, "this is the way we brush our teeth so early in the morning" and the verse would be followed by "the way we comb our hair" and, "the way we wash our face".

Our alphabets and numbers were written out on the blackboard and we would sing them out too, just as if we were learning a song. It was effective, but it might also account for the fact that we grew up with a kind of "singsong" way of speaking. Cursive writing was also on the backboard and we had to copy what we saw and most of us ended up writing just like Miss Hughes! Reading exercises were written out on the blackboard and we sang those too – together and individually until everyone got it right. Miss Hughes made sure that none of us left her class below grade level. So, it was a very big deal if you were "promoted" (There was no such thing as "social promotion"). It was quite a stigma not to be promoted, but those who had to repeat a grade did so with amazing acceptance. The darling among our teachers was Miss Fredna Wise – which she was. Miss Wise was the other homegrown educator. She taught third grade. Whereas the other teachers would not hesitate to paddle an unruly or sassy child - and that included the very lovely Miss Hughes, - Miss Wise never did. She understood that you had to search for the causes of the behavior and work to help the student become better adjusted. She never raised her voice and always spoke with a smile. First and second graders worked hard to get promoted so that they could be in her class and her own students accepted their promotions with timid reluctance. The fourth grade teacher was Miss McDuffy. She was barely bigger than the smallest child in her class, but she made up for it by being what we considered extremely mean. She did not hesitate to whip any child who was the least bit wayward or did not bring in the assigned homework, of which there was plenty. As for Mr. Hill, he was also a stern disciplinarian who took seriously his responsibility to prepare us for high school, in our case, Fessenden Academy. He taught the fifth and sixth grades.

One last word about our teachers: They were extremely proper in and out of the classrooms. Both Miss Hughes and Miss McDuffy lived in Ocala - both in the residential area of Broadway. Walking up and down Broadway, we would occasionally see them sitting on their respective porches and we would treat them with great deference, and they would reciprocate. However, you would never see them at the movies, in the dance halls or jukes and not even buying fish sandwiches at Buddy Bee's. Like Caesar's wife, they remained above reproach!

When we graduated from Union Elementary School, we were absolutely ready for Fessenden Academy.

Secondary Education in Zuber In the mid-1940's, the concept of Junior High School had not yet come to Marion County. Union Elementary School took us only through the sixth grade and then we were ushered into high school. In our case, the high school was Fessenden Academy; an expensive private preparatory school located less than three city blocks from Union. Although Fessenden was designed to accommodate residential students, an exception was made in our case. We could attend as day students up until the final year of high school at which time we were expected to move on campus. Even so, we had to pay the same tuition fees that all students paid. If this was an extra financial burden for our low income parents, we could not tell because somehow, without the slightest indication of being stretched to the limits, year after year, the tuition was paid and by the senior year, parents found the money to move us on campus.

At 12 years old, we certainly were not high school ready – few 12-year olds are. Fessenden administrators understood and prepared for this. What would have been 7th and 8th grades were designated Preparatory 1 and Preparatory II – meaning that we were being prepared to enter high school. In retrospect, I see the wisdom and tremendous insight into this educational approach. Maybe, this was a precursor to the much later concept of Junior High school.

I have spent my whole life in, and around educational institutions and I can say with absolute certainty that Fessenden Academy was no ordinary high school, beginning with its administration. Whereas typical high schools have only a principal, Fessenden had both a principal and a director; the Principal was Mr. James Harris (who later became principal at the high school in Wilmington, N.C. that graduated the legendary Michael Jordan) and the Director was Mr. John Allen Buggs (who also headed the Marion County chapter of the NAACP and eventually became the Director of The United States Commission on Civil Rights). Most of our teachers lived on campus, with only one living in Zuber, Mr. Emmanuel Wheeler, who taught Manual Arts, and one driving in daily from Ocala, Mrs. Lucille Simms, who taught English.

The administrators at Fessenden reified the John Dewey philosophy of education: "Learn by doing." Therefore, this was a "hands-on" high school – concentrating on experimental methodology. We had no textbooks – just an up-to-date personal dictionary and an up-to-date library. There was liberal use of audiovisual aids – long before these were used as teaching tools. We had a well-equipped science lab, large enough so that each student had his/her own workstation, complete with Bunsen burners. Our manual arts shop was equipped with every conceivable tool needed to build a house. Our theater stage was a full-sized professional one, with real drawstring professional curtains and several full-size backdrop scenery props. We had a 300-acre farm with livestock, as well as 4-H Club gardens. Culinary arts were taught in a professional kitchen and, like manual arts, both males and females were required to learn these skills. We had one of the first indoor gymnasiums in Marion County and several outdoor basketball courts, making Fessenden an ideal location to host regional tournaments.

Just as there were no 7th and 8th grades, there were no 9th, 10th, 11th, or 12th grades and there were no alphabet grades such as A, B, C, D, or F. Neither were there promotions at the end of each school year. (I know this requires a lot of explaining and I will do my best): Every school year began with three days of rigorous testing. The batteries of tests were used not only to measure achievement, but also to determine the cohort in which to place a student. The thinking behind this was that students learned better and quicker when they are academically on the same level. Also, it was to help the educators better judge the educational needs as well as the educational gaps of students. Whereas the first two years were called Preparatories and the last four were called Surveys. For example, Survey 1 corresponded to 9th grade; Survey 11 would be the typical 10th grade and so on. It was possible to "skip" surveys, depending upon your test scores. However, no matter how well you did, you were required to spend four years in high school, even if it meant taking advanced courses, the thinking being that college readiness necessitated a certain level of maturity.

As mentioned before, there were no letter grades – just numerical ones, with six being the lowest and 10 being the highest. Any student receiving a six failed. However, it did not stop there. Every teacher who had to assign a grade of six had to put in writing all the things that he/she did to help that student learn. No student could remain at Fessenden if it was determined that he/she could not or would not do what was required to remain on grade level.

At Fessenden, education was not just academics. Every student was expected to engage in extracurricular activities and these proliferated: varsity sports, debating teams, creative dance, choir, French Club, Book Club, Drama Club, Culinary Arts

Club and more. (I played varsity basketball; was on the track team where I ran the 440 and did both the high jump and the broad jump; was the President of the Book Club and a member of the Drama Club and the French Club – and spent a lot of time visiting the Culinary Club because of the samples they always shared)!

Social, cultural, and spiritual education were also integral parts of the Fessenden educational package. There were weekly seminars that required attendance and Mr. Buggs talked to us as if he were our parent. He advised us to date, but not to "go steady." He advised that we were too young to commit to each other and that a serious love affair at our age would retard our educational development. He also taught the importance of respect – not just respect for others, but for self as well. Once a week, we had vespers and attendance was mandatory. It was a solemn occasion where we sat quietly and meditated and would sing old fashioned spirituals and hymns. There was no preaching or proselytizing. At the last day of school before the Christmas break, Mr. Buggs would call an assembly and read the entire Dickens's <u>A Christmas Carol.</u> It didn't matter that it would put some of us to sleep – including me. The administration was big on cultural arts. Mrs. Zara Gale Buggs was the drama teacher. She was the daughter of the actress, Zara Cully, who played George Jefferson's mother in the sitcom, "Moving On Up". Mrs. Cully would occasionally come to the campus and direct some of our stage plays. Important entertainers of the day would come to Fessenden. The child prodigy, Philippa Duke Schulyer performed for us just before her untimely death in a plane crash. Rosamond Johnson, a Floridian and the composer who wrote the music for "Lift Every Voice and Sing", also visited us –as did Mrs. Bethune and A. Phillip Randolph, the native Floridian who shared the stage with Dr. King during the "March on Washington". Our basketball team was coached by none other than the legendary Coach John McClendon, one of the first persons to play for Naismith, the creator of the game, and also, a Basketball Hall of Famer.

The students at Fessenden came from all over the country, but also from other countries such as the Bahamas, Cuba, Jamaica, and Nigeria. I was speaking with one of the last students to attend Fessenden Academy a couple of years ago and asked her about her experience at that school. Her remarks were: "If I died and went to Heaven and if it was not like Fessenden, I would know that I was in the wrong place"! She was expressing my sentiments.

My academic ticket to Hampton Institute: Being incredibly tall has considerable disadvantages but, more advantages. By the time I was 12, I had already reached 6'6" – just two inches short of my adult height. This meant that I was the tallest person in my class, indeed, in the entire school, including the teachers.

My mother, who was only semi-literate but endowed with incomparable wisdom, took time the time to explain to me that because of my unusual height I would attract unusual attention and that many people would feel uncomfortable with that and compelled to make stupid remarks – and even thoughtless jokes. She conditioned me not to take offense or feel embarrassed, but to walk tall and proud without being proud. (This is just one of the great lessons I learned from my unschooled mother). One of the results is that I make friends easily and I have never had a fight in my entire life – including the usual childhood kind. Incidentally, there were three of us in Zuber with that same height; the other two were Alzo Patterson and Clinton Tyler. Both died in their early adult years.

Despite the expense, my family found the means to enroll me at Fessenden Academy, and to move me onto campus during my final year as was required. The goal was for me to complete high school and get a job that did not require me to spend my life engaged in menial employment. Although I studied hard and was a consistent honor roll student, there was absolutely no thought of ever going to college. During my sophomore year, Fessenden hired a new basketball coach. He took one look at me and decided then and there that he had found himself a Shaq! Until then, I had never even held a basketball. (All my time was spent studying and reading fiction, especially Russian, French, and English novels). The coach said to me: "If you play basketball for me, I can guarantee that you will go to college." He did not have to repeat it! However, he would have to teach me –beginning with the very basics. I worked hard every day learning the game and when basketball season began, I was the starting center. I also joined the track team and ran the 440, did the high jump, and the broad jump. I was in top physical condition. With the sight of going to college in my mind, I lived with a basketball in my hand and during my senior year, Fessenden Academy received its first, and only, invitation to participate in a statewide basketball tournament, which was held in Tallahassee. Recruiters from nearly all the African American colleges were on campus. We did not reach the finals, but neither were we eliminated in the first round. But I did myself proud! I made 85 points in a single game and received 17 full scholarship offers.

Now, the problem for me was choosing which offer to accept – not knowing anything about any of those colleges. I found a map and looked for the college that was farthest from Zuber. It turned out to be Hampton Institute. And it turned out to be the best choice I could possibly have made.

For us in Zuber, Virginia was up north, and we made no distinction between that state and, let's say, the New England states – anything north of Jacksonville in fact, was up north and up north meant cold weather, period. No one in Zuber had ever seen an overcoat and I would clearly need one and Sears and Roebuck did not carry the size I would need. There was an African American tailor in Ocala on Broadway – the only Black business east of Magnolia. We took a catalogue to him and asked him to make an overcoat for me. He had never seen, let alone made, an overcoat. Mama pleaded with him and said that she would supervise the project – which she did. To say the least, it was a doozy! To this day, my classmates at Hampton derisively remember that coat!

Not only was I uncommonly tall, I had feet to match! Now, we had the problem of finding presentable shoes that would fit me. The only place in Ocala that had shoes my size was a store called "The Hub," the only white owned store on Broadway west of Magnolia. Mama selected a genuinely nice pair of shoes and handed the owner $2.00. He politely, but firmly told her that the shoes cost $6.00. She informed him that her son was off to college and that he must have those shoes and, anyway, $2.00 seemed like a fair price. Mama refused to relent, and the owner finally let us have the shoes for $2.00. When I came home for the Christmas break, I happened to walk by the store and the manager saw me and ran out to call me in. He asked if I had passed all my subjects and when I told him that I had, he handed me a pair of new shoes. After that, he gave me a new pair of shoes every year until I graduated.

I cannot tell you who was more excited, Mama or me. It still amazes me that not once did Mama indicate a concern about me leaving home for the first time. At 17, I would be going away to a strange place and living with people who I had never met.

On September 2, 1950, I boarded the Silver Meteor heading north to Virginia. I had two suitcases full of new clothes and two shoe boxes filled with fried chicken, fried porkchop sandwiches, a few hard boil eggs, two apples, several slices of pound cake, and several slices of sweet potato pie. As the train pulled away from Ocala, both Mama and I knew that I was leaving home forever. I held back the tears until I could no longer see stoic Mama, standing alone on the platform with her arms folded and her head bowed in solemn prayer.

2: HAMPTON INSTITUTE: MY HOME BY THE SEA

In 1950, Negroes, as we were called then, were not allowed to use the dining car on the Silver Meteor that was taking me to Richmond where I would change to the B&O for Hampton. (The white people had no way of knowing that I would not have used it anyway. There was no way we could have afforded dining car prices. Besides, I doubted that they would have had fried porkchop sandwiches or homemade sweet potato pie)! That is why Mama had packed that mammoth meal!

Mama had stressed that I should do everything possible to avoid "a death of cold" and we had already decided that any place north of Jacksonville would be "up north" and, therefore cold, period! She made me promise to put on my new overcoat, which I did. So, you can imagine me strolling on the campus with a suitcase in each hand and wearing an overcoat in 90-degree weather and looking like six o'clock or Ichabod Crane. I could not imagine why the students were laughing their heads off, as they say, and I kept on strutting! I could hardly wait to write Mama and tell her that we had made a mistake about the north and I told her that it was exactly like the south.

However, by November, I asked the Lord to Bless mama for having such great insight! I had never felt so cold in my entire life and now I could hardly wait to pull out that overcoat, the one I should have donated to the Smithsonian Museum. Not only was the coat full length, touching my ankles, it was form fitting. It was definitely the original maxi. No one at Hampton had ever seen such a spectacle and no one has ever forgotten it!

The first student I met when I arrived on campus was Bill Evans, a fellow basketball recruit who hailed from Connecticut. To celebrate our new status as emancipated minors, we decided to have our first alcoholic drank and we defied the laws of Virginia and went into a "Whites Only" bar in the City of Hampton. I had explained to Bill that he must do all the talking because they would think that we were Hampton students from the north and would not know about segregation. (At that time, you could not distinguish my own speech from that of Gomer Pyle or Forrest Gump.) So, we ordered a bottle of beer and a coke as a chaser –ugh! That was my first and last drink.

A full scholarship meant only room, board, and tuition. For books and other expenses, we were given our choice of campus jobs. Being from Zuber, I enjoyed eating. So, I opted to work in the kitchen at Virginia/Cleveland Hall, a cafeteria located in one of the female dormitories. I was introduced to two foods I have never even heard of – scrapple and rhubarb pie. I really enjoyed these new foods until I found out that rhubarb pie has never been anywhere near a fruit, but was merely made out of a plant! And as for scrapple, I found out that it was a combination of unidentified scrap meat and grain. It was hard to believe that I was actually in college and I was determined to succeed.

The day before the college was to close for the Christmas holidays, Mama Nizer, the maître'd in the Virginia/Cleveland cafeteria, called me into her office and presented me with a rather large box. She told me that it contained a caramel layer cake that she wanted me to take to Mama. I did not know what, if anything, I had done to deserve this gift. That was our first time eating such a delicious cake.

I have been known to squeeze a dollar until the eagle grins, as the saying goes. Even though I went into town practically every week to see movies, I had sense enough to put aside enough money for my roundtrip greyhound tickets to go home for the Christmas holidays. And I must tell you about that experience:

Face to face with Jim Crowism: This would be my first bus ride and I was so excited. However, the excitement did not last long. I was the first on the bus and took the seat right up front, the one across from the driver. He asked me to move to the back. I asked if this was the bus to Florida and he said that it was. I carefully explained to him that leaving Virginia constituted interstate travel and that there was a federal law that forbade discrimination in interstate travel. He was stymied and refused to start the trip until several white passengers complained. They did not seem to mind that I was sitting up front and all was well until we made a breakfast stop in Savannah. There was no restaurant for Negroes. So, naturally, I went in the white facility. Again, I had to explain the federal law before the waitress would take my order. However, it was when the other passengers were boarding the bus that my plate of food was brought to me. I knew that the idea was for the bus to pull off and leave me stranded. What they had not reckoned with is the fact that people from Zuber are not easily fooled. I had only $5.00, the money that I had saved for my taxi fare home. The meal cost $1.50 but I left the entire $5.00 on the table, grabbed the plate of food and a fork and explained that the extra money should cover the cost of the plate, fork, the meal, and a generous tip for the waitress and I ran and got back on the bus! (I left the surplus money so that they could not accuse me of theft).

Hampton: my other mother: I do not think there is a major university campus in this country that I have not visited. So, it is with a high degree of authority that I say that Hampton has the distinction of being the most beautiful. It sits on more than 300 acres of land on a peninsula and has lots of impressive evergreen trees to match its extensive and well-kept lawns. The buildings are a mixture of stately old and state-of-the-art new. But it was not the campus that endeared me to Hampton, it was the people.

When I arrived at Hampton, I was on longer a child, but not yet an adult. The people in charge of guiding its students into adulthood seemed to have understood this and spent much time teaching us things that were beyond the academics, but nevertheless, equally important. Dean Hawkins taught us how to shake hands as if we meant it, using a firm grip and actually looking the other person in the eye. Although our meals were served cafeteria style, we were taught how to select a balanced diet and we were encouraged to even come back for second servings of vegetables but no seconds of meat or dessert. We were taught to greet people as we passed them, acknowledging not just their presence but also their humanity. Certain professors would sit with students in the campus grill and discuss issues and politics. I felt right at home at Hampton.

However, there were two incidents that nearly caused me to voluntarily withdraw from Hampton when I was still just a freshman. All male students were required to take ROTC. I declined. That was a "no no" but I stubbornly refused. I explained that I did not believe in killing and that I did not wish to be killed. I also explained that I never signed up for the draft and, therefore, had no draft card. This presented a big dilemma for Hampton but to its credit, the matter was dropped. I guess they figured that if I could defy the U.S. government, they had better let it go at that. The other incident involved a white professor, Dr. Goethe, who taught political science. She was constantly using the term "you people" and at first, I was not sure if she meant "you people" students or "you people" Negroes. Then one day she made the mistake of clarifying her meaning. She was clearly stereotyping Black people. In Zuber, we understood racism from the Jim Crow law. but we had no experience with individual prejudice. And for a white woman, paid to teach black students, to be so blatantly racist was like a hard slap in the face. I took my books and walked out of class and straight to the President's office. His door was opened, and I did not wait for his secretary to announce me but walked right in and began to talk non-stop until I had vented my anger. He believed my observations, called her in, and did not renew her contract.

My scholarship was rescinded: I was brought to Hampton to play basketball, but I came to Hampton to get an education. I had assumed that the two goals were compatible, and they were during all of my freshmen year and most of my sophomore year. Soon that would change. Coach Herman Neilson was an adorable father figure and clearly understood that

Hampton was an educational institution that was designed to accommodate both. He scheduled reasonable practice schedules, one that allowed adequate time for study. Bill Evans and I had become the anchors of the five freshmen who played together as a unit and would be called into a game to relieve the starting five during several periods of the game – and we were quite effective. The next year, we became the starting five and we were even more effective. Coach Neilson was promoted to the position of Athletic Director and the new coach was Morehead, a stubborn dictator who did not seem to understand that he was teaching students and not paid professional athletes who made their living playing basketball. Even though we thoroughly enjoyed the game, we knew that it was an extracurricular activity, not our profession! For crying out loud, we had no profession and were trying to attain one!

Well, one day I called Coach Morehead to explain that I was studying for a rigorous exam and would be a couple of hours late for practice. He insisted that I forego study and be on time for practice. Now, adhering to an unreasonable demand from Mama was one thing, but I was not about to have the coach decide for me what was in my best interest, scholarship, or no scholarship. As it turned out no scholarship won! Morehead rescinded the scholarship even though I was his starting center. (I had not realized that the coach would be so mean, he was married to one of the nicest persons you would want to meet, Consuela Lee, Spike Lee's aunt, and my Fessenden music teacher. I nearly celebrated when she finally divorced him). This was toward the end of my sophomore year and I had resigned myself to accept the reality that I would leave Hampton without a degree, but there was comfort in knowing that two years of college would keep me from having to return to the bean fields.

Now, in Zuber we were taught to be particularly engaging with elderly people who seemed lonely. There was one white woman who lived upstairs in a two-story building near the front of the entrance to the campus. You would usually see her sitting on the front porch in a rocking chair, always alone. The first day I saw her, I went and sat on the steps and spent close to two hours with her. Her name was Maria Phenix, the widow of the next to the last white

President of Hampton. She had known the founder, General Samuel Armstrong and was still friends with the General's widow. She had also known the two major financial supporters, Huntington and Ogden, who came to the aid of this struggling nascent institution, the site where the first public reading of the Emancipation Proclamation was held. She was a delightful oral historian and I made it a practice to stop by and spend time with her practically every day. So, when I was packing up to leave Hampton forever, I went to say goodbye to her. Although she was 88 years old, she was sharp enough to remember that I had not been there long enough to be graduating and that was when I explained what had happened.

Talk about serendipity! She told me that she had a plan and that I could remain at Hampton until I graduated. She invited me to accompany her upstairs and she showed me a lovely suite that was adjacent to her apartment, explaining that she owned it and that I could have it rent free. She told me that she was not in the position to cover my tuition but that she had a plan for that too. She would contact her friend, Mary Armstrong (the General's widow), who ran a residential family summer camp in New Hampshire and arrange summer employment for me, which she did.

When I returned from New Hampshire to start my junior year, I had more than enough money for two semesters of tuition. Even so, Mrs. Phenix gave me an allowance of $10.00 per week. She also paid for my meal tickets to eat in the student cafeteria but said that I could be her guest in the faculty dining room when I decided that I wanted to do so. Additionally, she showed me a cedar chest where she kept $300.00. She explained that it was "emergency money" but if I needed some and she was not around, that I should take what I needed, but that I must tell her so that she could replenish that stash. Of course, I never needed any and would not have taken it even if I had needed money.

Mrs. Phenix was absolutely oblivious to race. I am not sure how that could be, but she was. When I think about this phenomenon, I tend to attribute it to the fact that she was born in Burma to missionary parents and did not come to this country until she was six years old. She grew up in New England and graduated from Coby College, being one of the first five females to attend this all male college. Her first and only real experience with the south was when she married George Phenix and moved to Hampton. To show just how oblivious she was, imagine this: to clean and keep house for us, Mrs. Phenix had two maids, both of whom she addressed as "Mrs." even though one was black. The black maid had no problem cleaning my suite but, as you can imagine, the white maid, even though a maid, would not lower herself to "clean up after no colored boy!" Mrs. Phenix politely asked her (and Mrs. Phenix was the epitome of politeness) if she was thinking about finding another job. She was not, and this colored boy from Zuber had a white maid in the Jim Crow south. Yet, another important incident that showed Mrs. Phenix to be blind to race: One day she asked me to accompany her to her bank in downtown Hampton. She told the banker that she wanted him to witness my signature because she was authorizing me to write checks on her account. The banker turned beet red and actually tried to talk Mrs. Phenix out of such a drastic move. She seemed totally unaware that his concern was racially motivated and simply that the "kind man", as she referred to him, had her best interest at heart. That is why she took the time to remind him that she was "up in age" and pretty much alone, except for me, her house guest. I quickly stepped in to say that she meant "house boy" and that I was her aide and that smoothed his feathers. (What people in Zuber lacked in money, they compensate for with commonsense and self-protection.) One last comment about MRS. Phenix and race. When Marian Anderson came to give a concert at Hampton, of course she would not be allowed to stay in the hotel in downtown Hampton. The university had planned for her to stay in Trustee House, which had a small impersonal apartment. When Mrs. Phenix heard about this, she invited Ms. Anderson to spend the two nights with us. Now, for another new experience.

The boy from Zuber in a tuxedo: I had never been to a Cotillion Ball. Indeed, I had never even heard of such a thing. Well, there was a girls' dormitory counselor who had a lovely, stately daughter, reaching nearly six feet tall. When Mrs. Rhodes spotted me, she knew that she had found the escort for Bettie Jean. Fortunately, at Fessenden, (my high School) we were taught the waltz and ballroom dancing. But even now, I do not know how Mrs.

Rhodes was able to find a tuxedo to fit my 150 lb., six feet eight frame. Bettie Jean, and I became instant friends and I am incredibly pleased to have been the person to introduce her to her lifelong husband, Leon Bennett.

I was fully active in all aspects of university life: I did not pledge to a fraternity at Hampton, although I had planned to pledge Alpha. However, the semester before I could pledge the fraternity, I decided to pledge to the social club, Omicron. I was unprepared for the hazing and promised myself never again to subject myself to such an undignified and practically brutal experience. Nevertheless, I know every word of the Alpha pledge and all the words to the Alpha hymn.

After my freshman year I worked in the kitchen and the Grill, two fantastic and fairly lucrative jobs: I worked with Mr. Ruben Burrell to help to produce the programs for the football games – with the sole responsibility of selling them, for which I got to keep half of the proceeds. The other job was right down my alley. I have always been extremely nosey and when I was offered the job of switchboard operator, it was like putting the rabbit in the briar patch.

Whenever I could, I listened in on all incoming and outgoing calls, but I had, and still have, the grace not to repeat to anyone anything I heard. (It was knowledge for the sake of knowledge and not for gossip).

Leaving my other mother: As for the students, one could not have planned a better cohort of siblings! Through the years, we have remained in touch – and with growing affection. Hampton produces an up-to-date alumni directory and I seldom travel without it. Whenever I visit a city where my classmates live, I always call them and, without fail, they proffer home hospitality. Just a couple of years ago, I emailed Cherry (nee) Dowling to say that I would be in D.C. and she wasted no time in rounding up Hamptonians who came from Virginia, Maryland, Delaware, New Jersey, and Washington to join me for a luncheon mini reunion.

As I was leaving Hampton to explore New York City, Mr. Davis, the comptroller, saw me waiting for a cab and asked if I was returning home. I told him that I was going to New York. He wanted to know if I had money and I proudly told him that I had $50.00. He said that $50.00 would not go far in New York. He said that there was left over scholarship money and he gave me the $350, and in doing so, he exemplified familial Hampton – a true Alma Mater, which in Latin means nourishing/kind mother.

Now, I was ready to make the transition from Zuber to New York City.

3: FROM ZUBER TO NEW YORK CITY

In May 1954, Mrs. Phenix, now 90 years old, asked if I would take her to Hempstead, N.Y. where she would spend her remaining years with her sister. She reserved a Pullman sleeping car for us and I needn't tell you about the dilemma that caused in 1954. The conductor compromised: I could share the accommodations with Mrs. Phenix; but I could not take my meals in the dining car – they would be delivered to me. (Mrs. Phenix, however, did not spend her remaining years in Hempstead, but returned to Hampton in less than a year where she spent her final 10 years).

For the young Gilbert Lancelot Raiford, the Marco Polo son of Zuber, Manhattan was the Alpha and the Omega! The marvel began when I first saw the impressive NYC skyline – with the majestic Empire State Building standing guard over a city that boasted of housing more than 8,000,000 people! I was still trying to take it all in when the entire city disappeared. The train had descended into a tunnel that runs under/ through the East River. Neither Mrs. Phenix nor I was prepared for this experience and our Pullman porter saw our confusion and explained that everything was all right, that we were in a tunnel and would soon see NYC again. This was my first subterranean experience. As you probably know already, there is not even a basement in Zuber. When the train pulled into Penn Station, it was hard for me to believe that it was actually inside of a building! Grand Central Station was, by far, the largest building I had ever seen, and every inch of it was covered with people! We could hardly move more than a very short halting step at a time. I grabbed Mrs. Phenix by the hand because I was convinced that if we ever got separated, it would be forever. I directed the porter to find us a taxi and load it with our bags, which he did, and we were on our way to Hempstead. Hempstead is on Long Island and I quickly deposited Mrs. Phenix so that I could rush back to Manhattan where my maternal uncle and his wife were expecting me.

Aunt Sadie, truly one of a kind: Uncle Julius and Aunt Sadie lived on the second floor of a six-story walk up. The legendary, Ruth Brown, lived on the third floor. (She was living there when she recorded "Mama! He Treats Your Daughter Mean." which was very true!). Frankie Lyman and a small group of

African American and Puerto Rican boys crowded the steps every afternoon and evening, after leaving Stitts Junior High, making all kinds of noise, on their way to fame. I believe Frankie was about 12 then and would only live to be 25. (I was no longer living in that area when he died, but I did go to his funeral).

The area where we lived is called Washington Heights and is located just above Harlem. We were just four blocks from the Audubon Ballroom where Malcolm X was assassinated. In fact, I was on my way to hear him speak when I witnessed all the commotion surrounding the ballroom. So, I never got to see Malcolm.

My aunt Sadie was a real character! She informed me right away that I would be paying rent and making my own meals, explaining, "I am married to your uncle and not to you." (Fortunately for me, mama taught me how to cook even before I reached high school.) As for my uncle, he was a general building contractor and hired me to install insulation in the new houses. He paid me well and Aunt Sadie also received a "salary". I was shocked when she asked me to tell Uncle Julius to send her salary by me. I asked: "Do you actually get a salary?" Her answer: "but of course! Do you think I am going to wash his clothes, cook for him, keep his house, and sleep with him for nothing!?" She also asked if I played poker and I told her that I did not. (I don't think anyone in Zuber played poker. They played a gambling game called Georgia Skin, whatever that was.) Anyway, she said that I should meet her in the living room, and she would teach me – saying: "Bring your money." I asked if we could just play for fun and she advised me that: "Auntie plays nothing for fun my dear, bring your money." So, Uncle Julius paid me every Friday evening, but by Sunday, my dear Aunt Sadie had won back practically all of it - minus my rent and food money. However, justice would be served and there came a time when I paid her back, good and proper. But that is a story that must be told in the next chapter. However, I want to tell you now that in spite of all I have said about Aunt Sadie, she was one of my favorite people of all times.

Aunt Sadie introduced me to the Apollo Theater, where we went every Wednesday to see amateur night, where all or most of the rock-n-roll and rhythm & blues stars got their start. Because she loved to dance and Uncle Julius couldn't, Aunt Sadie took me to the Savoy Ballroom at least once a week. At that time, the Savoy was like a super Walmart - it never closed. It had, at any given time, three large bands in residence. These included such bands as Duke Ellington, Count Basie, Benny Goodman, Dizzy Gillespie, Lionel Hampton, and Max Roach. Cab Calloway, Sarah Vaughn, and Ella Fitzgerald were regulars. The bands played in eight-hour shifts – taking periodic breaks in between. The dance at that time was the Jitterbug, a very acrobatic dance where the female dancer was clearly thrown over the head of her partner and landed on her feet without missing a beat and nowhere was it more popular than at the Savoy. (As you must already know, there was no way that I could, or would, throw Aunt Sadie over my head – or anyone else for that matter!) White people from downtown and the suburbs frequented the Savoy but were contented to do the Lindy Hop because they were lost when it came to the Jitterbug. I joined them in doing the Lindy Hop.

In no time at all, New York City had become my home and during that time I could not possibly think of living anywhere else. I remembered asking Aunt Sadie if she had ever thought of leaving New York.

Her reply: "Leave New York? Where would I go"? She was expressing my sentiments.

4: FROM ZUBER TO UPSTATE NY AND CONNECTICUT

I had promised mama that when I graduated college, I would buy her a house in town. Well, there was no way I could accumulate enough money working for Uncle Julius and having Aunt Sadie win back my meager savings every weekend. I had to make a more sustaining arrangement. I applied for and got a residential counseling job in Esopus, New York at Wiltwyck School for Boys. Esopus is the kind of place that when you get there, there is no there! Still, it was a step up from Zuber. Anyway, there are four things worth mentioning about my one year at Wiltwyck: Because I had no living expenses and was not gambling with Aunt Sadie, I was able to save all my money and buy mama the house she wanted. One of the eight boys in my cottage was Salvador Agron who later became world infamous as the "Capeman" who murdered teenagers; my group and I were invited to Hyde Park to help Mrs. Eleanor Roosevelt celebrate her 73rd birthday. (A few years later, Mrs. Roosevelt and I were successful in getting the life sentence vacated against the redeemed Agron). On our days off, the counselors did not have to stay in the cottages with the boys. We had our rooms in a farmhouse and one night I found a copper head rattle snake in my bed. So I gave him (the snake) the bed, the room, and all my clothes and rushed to take the Hudson Line back to New York City! The only other thing of significance is that I went to Poughkeepsie one weekend and ran into one of my Hampton classmates, Leahgreta McKenzie. She was now a graduate student at Vassar and she encouraged me to continue with my education.

Yet another residential counseling job with wayward boys: Although I was back in New York City, I had definitely decided that I was not going to become re-employed by Uncle Julius. Within a week I had found another residential counseling job. The job was at Children's Village, an institution for "wayward teenage boys", located in Dobbs Ferry–on–the-Hudson. I was assigned to a cottage called Dwight, the only maximum-security facility in the compound. (I guess the thinking was that if I could handle the boys at Wiltwyck who were dubbed "Children who hate", then I should be ready for Dwight). Although all the doors and windows were kept locked, I did not see these young teenage boys as dangerous. Nightly, I would build a fire in the fireplace and we would all sit on the floor and make some popcorn, roast marshmallows, and I would tell ghost stories. The food was cooked in a common kitchen and brought to the cottages to be reheated and served. It was tasteless. On my first day off, I took the Hudson Line into Harlem and bought spices, ham hocks, collard greens, pork chops, cornmeal and flour. I returned that afternoon and made a good ole fashion Zuber dinner. Then, it occurred to me that I should ask if we could receive our portion of the food uncooked. Permission was granted and we began to eat well, and it was easy to see the change in the disposition of these boys. And because the institution's barber took a total of less than five minutes to give a haircut that would have shamed my dog, Homer, I bought some clippers and learned how to do it myself and asked the barber not to return. There are two things that stand out most about my experience at Children's Village: There was only a single white boy in Dwight. His incorrigibility was that he kept running away and had to be kept locked up. Anyway, the seven Black boys were quite mean to him and picked on him at every chance they got. So, one night when Joey Franks was taking his shower, I called a quick meeting of the boys and explained to them that any one of them could have been a Joey Franks, meaning the only Black boy among a group of whites and I invited them to think about how they would want to be treated. I also told them that I was planning to do something special for Joey and needed their help. The next day would mark his 16th birthday and I wanted us to give him a surprise birthday party (most of the boys had never had any kind of party and they were all excited by the prospect), I went into Dobbs Ferry and bought a huge birthday cake and a token gift. All the boys signed the card and I designated the biggest bully in the group to do the presentation. When the cake was brought out and we all started screaming the happy birthday song, Frank began to cry. He explained that he had never before had a birthday party. The other thing that happened almost got me fired: I was having a hard time accepting that these boys were locked up day and night. So, I had a meeting with them. I explained to them that I wanted to take them out to the basketball court so that they could have a little recreation. I made them promise not to run away (all of the boys in Dwight were notorious for running away). We were out there a couple of hours when, all of a sudden, a big squad of police cars came thundering into Children's Village with their Christmas lights flashing and sirens blasting! We were rounded up and taken back to Dwight – unceremoniously, I might add. I was not fired but chastised and since I do not take too kindly to that type of treatment, I resigned immediately and took a job in Stamford, Connecticut – getting farther and farther away from Zuber.

Recreation, using my Hampton minor: I was hired as the program director of the West Main Street Community Center but in practically no time at all I was actually running the Center. Also, I had gained a semblance of New York sophistication and no longer had a southern drawl. In fact, without due modesty, I think I pumped a little social life into placid Black Stamford. At the same time, Betty Brown, one of Hampton's beauty queens, had taken over the management of the YWCA in Greenwich and she also had developed a measure of sophistication and took over Black Greenwich – what little of it there was. Together, we did Hampton proud!

Rachael Robinson, the widow of Jackie Robinson, was chairperson of our board. I often saw her, but I never met Jackie. They did not live in town but in an area called The Ridges where all the homes were estates. I did meet one of his two sons, David, who was about four or five then. (The next time I saw David he was a grown man living in Tanzania and had made a trip here to visit his mother and to make a speech regarding coffee farming. He has a very successful coffee farm in Tanzania.)

Remembering what Leahgreta had advised me about continuing my education, I enrolled in the Graduate School of Social Work at the University of Connecticut, commuting twice a week from Stamford to Hartford. Then, one weekend I got it into my head to go to New York and visit Greenwich Village. When I ascended from the A Train at West 4th Street, I knew that my birth in Zuber had been a mistake; I had found my home. For the next five years, I would live my life as an authentic beatnik!

5: LIFE AS A "BEATNIK"

For people coming of age in the 1950's there were really only two places to be: Greenwich Village or the Left Bank in Paris –Haight Asbury would be added to the list later.

I was a little leery about settling in the Village alone. I would need a housemate. So, I began to cultivate the friendship of the 18 or 19-year-old Joe Johnson. (I was in my early 20's; meaning that there was not much age difference and his maturity or immaturity pretty much equaled mine.) Besides, Joe had a car, a stereo component set with every long playing jazz record you could find anywhere, and professional bongos – things we would need for our Village life, except for the car because it was a nuisance; there was never any place to park. Joe was a budding musician-a drummer.

It did not take us long to realize that we would never be able to afford the rents charged in the Village, So, we joined the pioneers who would create the East Village and rented an efficiency apartment at the affordable price of $35 per month. We lived at 314 East 6th Street in a six-story walk-up, on the second floor. Just one floor over us lived Laura

Richardson (a graduate of Hampton) and her sister, Sarah Jo. Altogether, there were 20 efficiencies in the building and two people around our ages inhabited all except one. The lone tenant was a Hampton transplant who, upon seeing me, smiled and said: "I remember you. You were at that little prep school in Virginia". (He was in a graduate program at Columbia University and quite pompous!)

This was the beginning of my social growth. Every day was a holiday and every night wa s a party. I cannot recall anyone in our building having a full-time job. Both Joe and I worked only on alternate weekends, meaning that we had very little money but we always had what we needed. When we were really short, we would have a rent party, and fairly wealthy people would come – just to be able to say: "I partied in Greenwich Village!" Joe's stereo and awesome collection of jazz records came in handy. The guests would leave us with enough money to last for several months.

Our clothing needs were minimal. We did not wear shoes but sandals in the summer and sneakers in the winter. My biggest expense was paying for the proliferation of courses I was taking at NYU. NYU is located just a few city blocks from East 6th Street and whenever I ventured on the campus, I would stop by to see what interesting courses I could take. I had no plans to matriculate or to graduate. I took courses as esoteric as Geopolitics; The Sociology of Religion; Cultural Anthropology; The World History of Economic Development; and the Evolution of Mankind. By the time I left the Village, I had accumulated nearly 100 graduate hours. There was not a single semester or summer when I was not in school.

Village life was an exciting life. In the beginning, most of our evenings and nights were spent in the various coffee shops scattered throughout the Village where we listened to poets such as Lawrence Ferlinghetti, Allen Ginsberg, and Jack Kerouac read their Beat Generation poetry. The typical cup of coffee at that time was 10 and 15cents, but in the coffee houses, the cost was 75cents. We gladly paid it but nursed a single cup all night long. Amiri Baraka, known as LeRoi Jones then, was married to Hettie Cohen and they owned a coffee shop in a sub-basement just two doors from where we lived. There Baraka would read his own poems and plays.

There were many new and exciting things to entertain us that were free. Foremost among them was the Cooper Union Cultural Arts Series. We went there to see the famous dance choreographer, Syvilla Fort, who brought her troupe down from Harlem and introduced us to our first experience with Afro/Cuban dances. Alvin Ailey, who was still dancing then and had not yet organized his own troupe, came there to perform, as did the great Nigerian drummer, Olatunja. But Cooper Union also sponsored great lecturers. My favorite among them was Dr. Margaret Mead, the anthropologist. Because of my love for anthropology, I often walked her to the subway, and we attracted unnecessary attention because she was barely five feet tall and I am six eight. (At that time, Mead was the curator at the American Museum of Natural History.)

To add more to our free cultural education, we often went to the Amato Opera House on the Bowery where we would watch the rehearsals of famous opera singers, including Maria Callas, and where I really learned to appreciate opera. I think Sarah Jo and I were into the classics much more than Joe and Laura. Not only did we experience opera for free, once we found out that tickets were not taken after intermission, we descended onto Broadway to see the last half of all the shows! On 42nd Street between Broadway and 8th Avenue, there were wall-to-wall movie theaters on both sides of the street. Laura and I would start on Monday and by Friday we would have seen every movie that was out. The matinee prices were .15 and .25 – depending upon arrival time and there was always a double feature, cartoons, and the world news. The movie theaters were also like the Super Walmart – always open!!

Then, there was jazz! Actually, it was the era of the big hitters. We lived one block from the Five Spot where Thelonious Monk was the musician in residence. He would arrive every afternoon around 4 p.m. in the limousine with Baroness Rothschild. Nightly, Monk would be joined by Miles Davis, Sonny Rollins, John Coltrane (a neighbor), or Dave Brubeck. We were there the night Miles first performed "Round About Mid-night". He was crying and so was the audience. Tito Puente was just getting started and we began to enjoy great Latin music.

W.C. Handy died when I was in the Village. I was determined to go to his funeral at Abyssinian Baptist

Church. When I arrived, the lines were around the block but I was determined to get into that church. Then, I saw Marian Anderson arrive in a chauffeur driven limousine. I rushed to open the door for her and told her that I had been assigned to escort her in. She remembered me from the time she performed at Hampton and stayed with Mrs. Phenix and me at Hollytree Inn. I had a front row seat!

There comes a time when one has to know when to move on. Armed with my Village education, I was ready for Europe. Paris, here I come!

6: FROM ZUBER TO EUROPE

One has to know when it is time to move on. There were so many places I wanted to see and so many things I wanted to do. Experiencing life outside of this country was one of them. A young African American engineer from New Rochelle who had been a guest in our flat, took it upon himself to give me a grand bon voyage party at a ballroom rental on West 14th Street. As for me, I had the urge to travel but not the funds to match that urge. Another young African American, one with whom I had worked in the summer camp in New Hampshire, had just received his scholarship money to attend the Yale University Law School. He gave me $1,000 of that money. However, I would need more. Remember, I was emerging from the life of a Bohemian, a life that did not include working. Also, remember dear ole Aunt Sadie? Well, I decided to try my luck with her and Uncle Julius. We had a weekend marathon poker game that was only interrupted when Aunt Sadie had to rush to an early morning church service. (I stayed put but prayed hard anyway!) By 4 p.m. on that Sunday, I had won $4,000 – all the cash they had on hand and then I had the nerve to ask Aunt Sadie to drive me to the airport.

I explained to her that I was going to Europe and she exclaimed: "With my money!" I respectfully said: "No, dearie, with my money. It used to be your money." She laughed and drove me to the airport.

Weeks before, I had reserved a bed and breakfast in London. I arrived late in the evening and was greeted by a West Indian maid who informed me that "madam has retired" and being from Zuber I just automatically thought she was telling me the lady no longer worked and I wondered why she thought that had anything to do with me. Anyway, she told me that I was to follow her into madam's "chamber" (In Zuber that translates to mean courtroom, but I kept quiet and did not display my ignorance!). However, when I entered the bedroom and saw madam decked out in a white flannel night gown and a hat to match, I could only think of Charles Dickens and before I could catch myself, I said: "Good evening Miss Havisham!" Anyway, London was not foreign enough for me. Therefore, I cut short my visit there and took the Orient Express to Paris, arriving at mid-night. This would be my first opportunity to use my Fessenden acquired French. I had never spoken the language with a native speaker and wasn't sure that I could.

However, I was daring. I found a coin telephone and, using my traveling bible, "Europe on 5 Dollars a Day". I selected an affordable pension and called to see if there was a vacancy. There was and I reserved it. I was told to take a taxi, but I was not about to squander my hard-to-come-by money that way. I asked for and received directions via the metro.

For some unknown reason, I was reluctant to embrace Paris. For three days, I stayed in my room or close by. On the fourth morning, I took the metro and ascended smack in the middle of the Latin Quarter. I was HOME. It is easy to fall in love with Paris at first glance. I spotted a group of African and Caribbean fellows right off. They were sitting at an outdoor café on Blvd. St. Michel and waved me over. It was the first of the many hours we would spend together solving the problems of the world and when I told them that I knew Coltrane and Miles personally, I became pivotal – and with that position came lots of hospitality. I immediately moved out of the pension and into the dormitory at the Sorbonne – which was cheaper, cleaner, and within walking distance of my Greenwich Village substitute. Naturally, I had to enroll as a student.

The Latin Quarter is not the world, meaning that I had to move on. I just had to see a bull fight. So, next stop Barcelona. Because I had the good sense to purchase a urailpass before leaving for Europe, I was traveling first class. Unlike the trains in the United states that have coaches, the European trains have compartments – small enclosed sitting rooms that can accommodate up to six people. I shared an apartment with a young Briton who had just received his law degree. The conversation revealed that neither of us had made hotel arrangements, meaning that we did not know where we would be going when we reached Barcelona, but I was not worried. I only needed to consult my traveling bible to arrange accommodations and we made the decision to become temporary roommates, my very first experience in sharing living space with a white male. We found a very quaint but also very clean, small hotel, located within easy walking distance to Las Ramblas. Las Ramblas is a very wide boulevard, with an equally wide promenade, reaching from downtown to the seaside. My new roommate was only going to stay in Barcelona three days, and we spent practically all of those days walking up and down Las Ramblas, the socio-political center of the city.

However, I did not come to Barcelona to hang out with some white boy from England. I could hardly wait to see the bull fight, but I was not entertained. It was not a fair fight and no matter what, the bull had to die. While everyone around me was shouting "Ole, Ole!" I was crying and vowed never to see another bull fight – not even in movies. Of course, that did not stop me from going on to Pamplona to participate in the running of the bulls but I made sure that I was way in front of the crowd and the bulls would have to trample on a lot of people before they got to me!

After the Briton left, I was alone, but not lonely. There is a paved park at the beginning of Las Ramblas, and I went there to watch the local people dance. Four teenage boys came up to me and asked if I wanted to join the dancing -they would teach me the folk dance. As you already know, people from Zuber do not squander an opportunity to dance. I was quite oblivious to the fact that I was the only black person in town and easily the skinniest and the tallest, but none of this prevented me from thoroughly enjoying myself.

The park closes at midnight. One of the boys asked if he could walk me to my hotel. He said that he wanted to talk to me about America. His use of English was as limited as my use of Spanish, but we were able to communicate effectively. I invited him to be my guest for lunch the following day. In the spirit of reciprocation, he invited me to dinner with his family. I discovered that they were poor. His father was the breadwinner, but he was not winning much bread. His monthly salary was 2000 pesos, which translated to mean about $20. I thanked them profusely for their hospitality and, as I was leaving, I slipped Manuel's father $20.

On my way back to Paris, I met nine young Americans who convinced me to get off the Paris bound train and go with them to Rome; saying that the opera "Aida" was going to be performed on the stage of the old coliseum amphitheater. There was no way I was going to miss that but, since we had a couple of days to spare, I enticed the group to get off the train on the French Rivera because I had never been to a casino and wanted to try my luck at Monte Carlo. A bad choice – didn't win a thing.

When we got to Rome, I took charge of the group and using my traveling bible, I was able to find a pension where we could all stay together for the affordable price of $1.50 per night, which included breakfast. The opera was fantastic, and I went to see it every night I was in Rome and everyday was spent in the Sistine Chapel and walking on the Appian Way and touring the catacombs.

My next stop would be Zurich, but I needed to return to Paris to collect my mail at the American Express office. That is when I ran into James Baldwin. I had a copy of <u>Another Country</u> with me and he was delighted to see I was reading his book. He was giving an international party in Marrakesh and asked if I wanted to come. Definitely not. I was still just up from Zuber and certainly not ready to hang with the big boys.

I had many adventures in Europe and visited 13 countries and shared accommodations with 35 different people, from nearly the same number of countries, including whites from America – people I had never seen before and never saw again. (When your money is tight, you cannot be but so choosy and you would pay only half when you shared a room.)

I must tell you about this one adventure: The U.S. Dept. of State warned all of us that were traveling in Europe that if we had to go to Berlin, we should definitely not take the train because that city was an enclave inside of Communist East Germany. I had a Urailpass so why should I have to spend all that money to fly into Berlin. When I went to make my reservation, the ticket agent asked if I had a visa to visit East Germany. I explained that I was not visiting in East Germany, just passing through. He said that I would still need a transit visa. I told him that his job was to make my reservation and not worry about my visa situation. He quietly made the reservation but not without adding "it's your funeral" and that nearly came to pass.

I was in my compartment with the door locked when an abrupt stopping of the train awakened me. It was past midnight, and it was storming outside. Then, I heard thunderous banging on the door. I opened it and there stood a gladiator type woman with a machine gun pointing at me and asking to see my visa. Behind her were three men – all with drawn lugers. I gave her my passport and pretended that I had no idea what she meant. I decided to use the race card. I told them that they were persecuting me because I was Black. They went into a huddle and decided to sell me a transit visa on the train. That postponed the problem but did not solve it. (You will have to wait for the next installment. For all our meekness, people from Zuber can be awfully hardheaded and stubborn! You shall see.)

TO EUROPE II

In the late 1950's and early 1960's, West Berlin was the place to be if you were young and trendy. Even though I had only one of the qualifications, I was determined to make the best of it. I was staying not too far from the Am Zoo, one of the most famous zoos in the world at that time, and I spent most of my afternoons there. The evenings were spent at a nightclub where each table had a telephone and, invariably, someone would call my table to invite me over to join the party at another table. You see, being 6'8" and ebony, I was exotic! Being in West Berlin was exciting, but I was just as interested in seeing East Berlin. The U.S. Department of State had warned all Americans not to dare this on their own, that we should go as an intourist (with an official guide), which I did. Immediately after crossing Check Point

Charlie into East Berlin, I was in another world. It was drab and dreary, and the people seemed only to exist, not to live. I only spent a day there and when I returned to West Berlin, I ran into a group of young people who were heading to Helsinki for the International Youth Conference. I was determined to make that conference but the problem was my visa was good only for leaving Germany via the route I took to get to West Berlin, meaning that I would have to go south and Helsinki was north. I could not possibly make the conference if I had to go south first. I thought I could trick the conductor and made reservations for the train going to Helsinki. When I tried to go through the gate, the conductor saw that my visa did not permit me to travel north and he suggested that I wait a few hours until the offices opened and buy an appropriate visa. I thanked him and said that I would, but I had no intentions of doing so because the next train would not leave until the next day. The station was like Grand Central in NYC and Union Station in D.C. - with over a dozen gates. I casually walked down to the farthest gate, flashed my bogus visa, and rushed to get on the train. It worked – well, partially anyway. Less than a mile from the border, the train stopped. The Gestapo people were not so kind this time. They actually made me get off the train and wait on the platform six hours for a train to take me back to Berlin.

I eventually got to Helsinki, but by this time, the conference was over. However, there was still a group not yet ready to return to their respective countries and they were headed for Russia. I decided to join them. The price was great. For $50, I was able to get a cruise from Helsinki to St. Petersburg, a bus to Moscow, and two weeks hotel stay that included all meals. However, I would have to go as an intourist – meaning that I would have to be escorted everywhere I went. At first, I did not mind that. Later, I decided that I really wanted to explore on my own. That opportunity presented itself early one morning when I opened my door and found the agent asleep. I sneaked passed him and took the service elevator to the basement and exited the hotel unseen. I went into the first subway station I could find and rode to the end of the line. One of the first persons I saw was a Black man. I had memorized a few Russian phrases and I struggled to recall them as I greeted the man. He started laughing and said: "You can speak English. I'm from Brooklyn". He wanted to know what I was doing in Russia and why was I not with an escort. I told him the truth. He admonished me but said that he could probably spare me any serious repercussions, which he did. He was some kind of minor official. I spent the whole day with him and his Russian family.

On my way back to Paris, I decided to stop by Bamberg, Germany where my housemate of my Greenwich Village days was stationed. I arrived at midnight and once again, had not made any sleeping arrangements. I was a college graduate, and I knew that college graduates were usually 2nd Lieutenants. So, I took my chances. I told the sentry guard that I had just been transferred and that I needed a place to sleep and that he must show me how to get to the officers' quarters. It worked. The next morning, I set out to find Joe and I talked him into asking for a two-week pass so that he could come with me to Paris. That worked too. However, when we arrived in Paris and I collected my mail from the American Express office, there was a letter from a friend that I had made in Barcelona, inviting me to return to Spain and join him in Costa Bravo where he had the use of a villa for two weeks. I taught Joe a few useful French phrases and I was off to Spain again. However, I was not going to spend that much time in one place. So, after a few days, I was off to Scandinavia. My first stop was Sweden where I found nice and affordable accommodations on a student boat that was anchored at a pier in the downtown area of Stockholm. Although I was really enjoying my stay in Stockholm, I could hardly wait to get to Copenhagen and go to Tivoli Gardens, at that time the most famous theme park in the world – built even before Walt Disney was born. I was not disappointed. As amusement parks go, Tivoli was in a class all by itself. I spent several days in, again, Copenhagen, but I was anxious to visit the Land of the Midnight Sun – the northern most part of Norway. Train travel through the fjords is absolutely breath taking! I arrived in Bergen around 12 o'clock but I couldn't tell if it was a.m. or p.m. because the sun does not set in northwest Norway in the summer. I had made no arrangement for accommodations, again, yet I was able to find a bed and breakfast for $2.00 per night in the home of a widow and her two children, including a son who was a college freshman at the University of Bergen. He told his English Language professor that they had an American houseguest who spoke "perfect English". I was invited to accompany him to class for a week and speak in English, for which I would be paid $50. I still had somewhat of a southern drawl and sounded very much like Gomer Pyle and Barney, but I made the much needed $50.

Now, it was time to return to the real world. I was not yet 30, but I needed a job and a family. I returned to New York City with my bachelor's, two masters ,50 in my pocket and I was homeless. Joey Franks, the former juvenile delinquent who I had befriended when he was 16 years old and an inmate at Children's Village, would rescue me.

7: THE BEGINNING OF THE END OF MY VAGABOND DAYS

Now, gainfully employed and having satisfied much of my yearning for adventure, I made the decision to become a responsible adult. This meant that I would, for the first and only time in my life, establish a home where I would be the sole occupant. I found a newly renovated kitchenette at 25 Clinton Street – in the heart of the Lower Eastside. Aunt Sadie came down to help me get settled. She went to the Garment District and bought some impressive material and made me a magnificent bedspread and matching draperies. I had purchased a wall-to-wall carpet, and a nice stereo-component set. Having established my home, I was ready to meet my neighbors.

On my first night there, I wandered out in the street where there was loud music and lots of chatting. I wanted to join the festivities. As it turned out, I had moved smack in the middle of a Puerto Rican neighborhood – infested with a youth gang called The Young Lords and they had just returned from having a "rumble" with a street gang in Harlem. My appearance brought the festive mood to a halt and eight teenagers with bats and chains confronted me.

They surrounded me and wanted to know why I was in their neighborhood. I kept smiling and told them that I had just moved in and that I wanted to know where things were, such as grocery stores and laundry machines and if they would be kind enough to assist me, I would be forever grateful. I also said that I would buy two six packs of beer and we could go to the park and talk – giving one of them a five dollar bill and telling him that he must return to me all of my change. It was done. We talked until nearly 4 a.m. and I asked them to walk me to my building and to meet me there the next evening when I returned from work and that I would make dinner for them.

All eight of them were waiting in front of the building when I reached home. Inside the apartment, they were profuse in their admiration. I made a spaghetti dinner which we eat heartily, and I put them out around midnight. They expressed much happiness that we had become friends. When I returned home from work the next evening, my door was ajar. I had been burglarized! Gone were the bedspread, the draperies, all the sheets and pillowcases, the stereo set, the carpet, and the food. Only my clothes were left alone. I had never been so furious! I actually went looking for those Young Lords (clearly a misnomer! Young Devils would have been more descriptive)! I could not find a single one of them anywhere. For three evenings, I canvassed the neighborhood but no Young Lords. One week later when I arrived home, three of them were sitting on the steps. They greeted me in the manner of long-lost friends, saying: "Gil, man, where you been? We's been lookin' all over for you". I told them that I had been looking for them too and left it like that. Then I invited them to join me for dinner. I had not replaced anything that had been stolen but had bought a cheap radio that provided us with the music of the night. Not a word was spoken about the now fairly empty apartment. By the end of the week, all eight members had returned, and we had dinner together every night for the next two weeks. I had become attached to these wayward boys and knew that I had to do something to guide them into a meaningful future. So, one night I turned off the radio and said that I was calling a meeting. I asked each of them to tell me what his plan was for the future, explaining that they would all be adults in one or two years. No one had a plan. I told them that even though they were school dropouts, I could prepare them for college and could possibly get full scholarships for them based on their level of poverty. They consented to be tutored for the G.E.D. It took about a month to prepare them for the test. In the meantime, I went to NYU and secured full scholarships – knowing that the university had "War on Poverty" contracts. Seven of them passed the exam, with six passing the first time. The eighth one could not pass, but I was able to get him into a trade school where he learned auto mechanics and spent his adult life working for the NYC Transit Authority, reaching the status of supervisor, and retiring a few years ago. The others became college graduates and several of them have retired to Florida where at least two of whom live in Marion County, the same county where Zuber is located.

The Marco Polo of Zuber settles down, well, sort of: After gallivanting over 13 countries in Europe, I returned to NYC with only fifty cents – and without a job and without a place to stay. I am so grateful that the Lord really does look out for babies and fools! On my way from the airport, as I mentioned before, I ran into Joey Franks, the white juvenile delinquent from Children's Village but now a respectable and gainfully employed man. He had just gotten married to an extremely attractive Argentinian and told me that they were living in the Bronx. He was appalled to discover that I was basically homeless, and the couple invited me to stay with them. The place turned out to be an efficiency apartment with a single bed and a sofa, all in one room. Obviously, it did not take us long to figure out that this was not going to work! Within a week, Joey had found another place for himself and his new bride. He paid a month's rent for me and bought a liberal supply of groceries. He also gave me a handful of subway tokens and wished me well.

It turned out that I did not need the month's grace period after all. The day after they moved out, I read an employment ad where the job included an apartment and all meals. The catch was, it was a residential position that called for living and working with white male teenagers. I really did not expect to get the job, but I was bold enough and desperate enough to apply anyway. When I arrived for the interview, there were three other applicants – all white males. When I was told that I had been accepted, it took me some time to really believe it! It turned out to be the kind of job I would have paid to do. I was charged with enhancing the educational and cultural growth of eight extremely bright teenagers who had grown up in various foster homes and institutions. I was required to take them to Broadway plays; the opera, concerts, lectures, on vacations, and to help them with their college courses. I also taught them basic etiquette; things that had been taught me at Fessenden. In return, I received a completely furnished apartment and a small salary. I also received maid and laundry services as well as three very delicious meals a day. However, I could not think of this as a career. It was only a respite. I just needed to catch my breath and put my life on course. I had not lost sight of the fact that I wanted a wife and family, and this was absolutely no way to get either. I had to find a real job and get a real life.

The New York City Department of Welfare was hiring. I took and passed the civil service exam and arranged to work at my live-in job without pay, just room and board –which included a daily sack lunch. However, I found that I was still not ready to behave myself like normal people. I simply refused to punch the clock. I saw that as impugning my integrity. Also, a standard 9-5 did not make sense to me. I reasoned that if you had a job to do, you did it until it was finished. It might take eight hours, or it might take more or even less. When I received my caseload, I began to work on it immediately and seldom did it take me eight hours a day to get all my work done. Also, coming in a 9 a.m. did not work for me. When the janitors came in to open up at 6 a.m., they would find me waiting and when my supervisors would arrive, my desk would be nearly clean and I would be waiting for any additional cases that had not been assigned. If there were none, I would leave and go to see a movie or read a novel. This did not sit well with the Department of Welfare. Except for the work that I was doing, there was no record of me being in its employment, meaning that I could not expect pay. That did not especially bother me in the beginning because I still had room and board and I could walk to work, and I had enough savings for incidentals. However, I began to think seriously about getting married and I would have to find my own apartment. I was working full-time but stone broke! That didn't really bother me too much either because I was working in an agency that helped people who were broke. So, I submitted my application to receive welfare. When the intake worker saw that I had all those degrees, she wondered why I was not employed, and she was practically in shock when I told her that I was a caseworker with the Department. She thought it was some kind of a joke until I told her about the predicament. She called my supervisor who verified my employment. I was sent to Central Office to meet with Commissioner James Dumpson where I explained my aversion to punching a clock and to a standard 9 to 5. Dumpson, apparently impressed by my "outstanding" performance record, said that I would be assigned to another departmental position where I would not have to punch a clock. Incidentally, I received all of my back pay –which was considerable!

I was assigned to work in Family Court where I assisted judges in deciding child support cases. My job was to make an assessment of how much an absentee parent had to pay. Most of these defenders were hardly more than minimum wage earners and sometimes I would recommend that they pay nothing, mainly because whatever they paid would be deducted from the family's welfare check. And the absentee parent was financially unstable him/herself. You can imagine that I was, again, heading for trouble. In spite of the budget I presented to her, Judge Sylvia Liese, (obviously the model for Judge Judy) insisted upon issuing a payment order. I challenged her in open court and did not back down even when she threatened to hold me in contempt – which she finally did, and my supervisor had to come in and get me out of custody. The only Black judge on that court was Jane Bolin, a real classy lady and an excellent judge. She was the first African American female judge in the entire U.S. (she died about seven years ago). After that run in, Judge Liese and I carefully tiptoed around each other. However, knowing that she had money, our lukewarm relationship did not stop me from asking her to give me $1500 to send one of my drug addicted friends to a Synanon treatment center in California. To her everlasting credit, she gave me the money.

Now, I had a paying job and an apartment, and I was quite ready for marriage. Whether or not marriage was ready for me, we shall see.

When I reached my 30's, it was time for me to start my family. I had met Mildred Faulcon in the Rockywold-Deephaven camp a couple of years prior.

She had been my only titular girlfriend. We had spent a lot of time together on Asquam Lake as well as on top of Bear Mountain at night. She was and is a very beautiful person. She was still a student at Hampton and when she graduated, she returned to her home in Weldon, North Carolina. I was not at all certain that her proper family would accept this rootless vagabond, but I visited anyway and took a hotel room in town. Her family accepted me immediately; at least that is my impression. When Mildred took a teaching job in Elizabeth City, N.C., I visited her and also took hotel accommodations. She visited me at 25 Clinton Street, and she took a room at the Barbizon Hotel for Women just off Central Park. In a nutshell, we did not cohabitate before we were married in June 1962 in Rocky Mount, N.C.

Our first Child was Janice, then Wanda, and then Lance. They were born two years apart. There was a hiatus of about 10 years before our last son, Douglas, was born. We had to decide how to raise children. We would not use punishment to teach expected behavior but verbal communication instead. We would not shower them with gifts but give one very thoughtful gift at Christmas and on birthdays. We would not yell at them and certainly not call them hurtful names out of anger. We would avoid saying "no" and would never say it without a thorough explanation and would even entertain a rebuttal. We would read to them and encourage reading by them. We would stress honesty and trust and we have never had to hide money from them. All of them have always had access to or could gain access to Mildred's and my bank account, which has always been a joint account. All of our children have college degrees and no prison record. As for Mildred, I could not have picked a better wife with whom to spend the rest of my life. A couple of weeks after we were married, I took her to Ocala to introduce her to my family. They accepted her with great gusto. Both Mildred and I had accumulated savings and we used our combined money to take Mama furniture shopping. I think Mama thought that there was plenty more where that came from because she selected very expensive stuff, especially the dining room furniture, which is still in excellent condition today; 53 years later.

In time, we would leave the glamor of NYC for the cultural wilderness of Kansas

8: FROM ZUBER TO LAWRENCE, KANSAS

By the mid 1960's the "War on Poverty" was a reality and many of us benefitted from it. In my case, it took the form of a full and liberal scholarship. I was among more than a dozen African American students who were admitted into the Masters of Social Work program at NYU. We were to choose from three majors: casework, group work, and community organization. I could not choose and ended up with a triple major, which earned me the derogatory title of "Super N..." Also, I was not an easy student to teach. Dr. Arthur Katz was one of my professors and considered himself an expert on race. I challenged him on every point and the class practically divided into a debate between Katz and me.

There were enough of us at NYU to organize an Association of Black Social Work Students. The irony in this was the fact that Cenie Williams headed the association. He was a South Carolina Geechee, with speech that only resembled English, but what he lacked in verbal skills he more than compensated for by his commitment to race and by the bold ideas that flowed from him. We became instant friends and although Cenie was far from studious, I was determined to see to it that he graduated. One night he called me at 1:30 a.m. and asked me to meet him at an all-night café. He told me that he did not like or support the perspective that many of the professional Black Social workers had regarding NABSW. His position was that they viewed it in the same way as their white counterparts. He proposed that we take over the organization. He suggested that we use what we had learned about community organizing and put it into practice. We did, and it worked, and Cenie became president of the National Association of Black Social Workers and I became his speechwriter.

Upon the attainment of my MSW, I yearned to teach. Although I was still with the NYC Department of Welfare, I thought I would seek a position as an adjunct and there was no better place to seek such a job than at NYU where I had received degrees. I went from department to department, but no one would hire me. I decided that I would complain to President James Hester and went to his office without an appointment but would not be put off by his receptionist who insisted that I needed one. I parked my lanky frame on a sofa and waited for the President to leave for lunch and when he did, I joined him stride for stride, pleading my case as we walked. I practically insisted that the university honor its degrees by giving me the opportunity to teach there. He promised to get back to me and he kept his promise, and I was hired to teach my first college course, Sociology 101. I really could teach, and I really enjoyed it.

By this time, I had moved up rapidly in the NYC Department of Welfare and was making a good salary. My plan was to stay with the Department and teach a course on the side. Then, out of nowhere came a totally unexpected call from Arthur Katz, the professor whose academic life I had made miserable. He had been appointed Dean of the School of Social Work at the University of Kansas and he was asking me to leave NYC and the Department of Welfare and come to teach for him in Lawrence, Kansas. He offered me a salary comparable to what I was getting and promised that I would have to teach only three courses a semester and that they would meet only once a week. That was the clincher. I could not imagine a better world where I would be making a living wage and still have all that free time! Of course, I was also hired to recruit minorities to the university

– which also suited my lifestyle, plus, there was all that free travel with a liberal per diem. Although this was to be my first appointment as a full-time faculty member, I would not start as an instructor, but as an assistant professor.

In a faculty of 25, Henrietta Waters and I were the only African Americans – and both of us were feisty! Those 23 white folks had their hands full. Henrietta and I caucused every day, and before faculty meetings, we decided beforehand what our position would be on every issue. Every time we felt that our logical positions were being ignored, we would get up and leave the meeting and occasionally yell back over our shoulders "You white people do what you want", leaving them stymied. However, there were two incidents that demanded considerably more of us than just walking out of a faculty meeting:

Three young Black Panther Party members had gone into a white church and robbed everybody by making them place their wallets and all their jewelry in a pillowcase. Lawrence is not that big of a city and the police manned every exit. They could not escape. My family hid them in the fashion of the historic Underground Railroad and spent two days getting them to understand the gravity of what they had done. We promised to try to undo the damage. We learned that the robbery was committed to get money to relocate to Africa - not any particular country, (it was thoroughly misguided)! Anyway, we went to the police to say that everything that was taken was still intact and that we would help them locate the men and give everything back, but would do so only if we could remain with them throughout the arrest and arraignment process. We would put up our houses for bail as collateral and we had an agreement. Since they were college graduates, we prevailed open Dr. Katz to admit them to the School of Social Work on a full scholarship. This was also successful.

The other incident involved a young African American administrative assistant who had gone to Topeka and purchased a gun. Before he returned, to the campus, the storeowner had called the university and reported him, and he was summarily fired. White men in trucks kept driving by his house all that afternoon. Henrietta, her husband Bob, the lone African American professor of science, and I went to the young man's house and spent the night keeping watch – and with guns too! (Talk about the wild, wild west!). Fortunately, nothing happened but we still needed to help the young man get his job back. That was no easy task. Even though we pointed out all the white professors whose gun ownership posed no problem for the university, we could not prevail. They were forcing us to come "out of our bag", as the young folk say – and we did just that. It was the end of the school year, so, Henrietta and I decided that we would not turn in our grades and we convinced the science professor to follow suit – which he did. There would be no graduation ceremony that year. The young man was rehired.

As for the would-be Black Panthers, they came to me after one year was up and wanted me to assure them that the skills they were being taught could be used in Africa. Not being an expert in the transferability of social work skills, I went and asked the Dean. He wasn't sure. I told him that if he would keep me on full salary for the entire summer, I would go to Africa and find out. He did and I did. Do you want to know about my experience teaching social work in Nigeria?

9: FROM ZUBER TO AFRICA

The year was 1969 and black pride had become the rallying cry of the day. Lawrence, Kansas was the battleground for our social work students. One student, in particular, announced that he would not take another course that was taught by a white person and asked if I would organize "independent study" courses and teach him myself. Jim Renick was in his last year of the MSW program. I organized tutorials and taught him in his remaining five subjects. At that time, Jim was sporting an Afro that would have done Angela Davis proud! (In time, Jim would cut his hair, don a three-piece suit, and become Dr. Renick – and hold jobs as president of well-known state universities, one an HBCU, the other two predominantly white.)

As for me, I was still determined to go to Africa, but did not know how that could be accomplished. I had a wife, three small children, and no bank account – just determination and ambition. Then, I read an article about Operation Crossroads Africa and learned that that organization sent Americans to African countries every year to work as volunteers in rural villages. The volunteers were college students, but the group leaders were professional adults. The students had to pay $3200 for the privilege of doing menial work for free in rural African villages and under difficult conditions. Surprisingly, there were always more applicants than could be accommodated. But not so surprising was the fact that the vast majority of applicants were white. The founder and director of the program, Dr. Robinson, received over 200 applications from professionals offering to volunteer their time as group leaders. Like the students, they would get no pay but unlike the students, they did not have to pay. This suited me just fine, but there was absolutely no guarantee that I would be selected. Dr. Robinson said that he only needed 20 leaders. All of us had to submit application letters. We were told that only 50 people would be invited to spend a week with Dr. Robinson and his staff in a rural village in upstate NY. When the invitation came inviting me to be among the 50, I felt that I was a shoo in, but I had not reckoned that my qualifications were pitiful compared to most of the other invitees. Most of them were white and Ivy League graduates. Many of them majored in African Studies and several of them were already fluent in a variety of African languages. My Zuber experience was absolutely no match! I had to devise a plan to insure my acceptance. I decided to make myself useful. I was up every morning at dawn and went into the kitchen to help prepare breakfast. I also took the initiative to help keep our cottage clean and orderly. At the end of the week, Dr. Robinson read off the names of the selectees. Mine was first!

Now that it was fairly certain that I would be going to Africa, I had time to devote to my fears; chief among them was the battery of shots I had to take – 14! That produced great stress, but I survived them. However, my second, and equally devastating fear, was that of snakes and I knew they would be prevalent in a rural village. Fortunately, I was spared that confrontation.

Dr. Robinson had decided that along with a group of eight students I would be going to Nigeria. When the city officials in Lagos learned that I was, in real life, a college professor, they asked if I would consider teaching social work and advanced public administration to the staff at Lagos City Council. They did not have to ask twice! Also, instead of living in a rural village, the officials arranged for us to live in compounds on the campus of the University of Lagos.

Our meals would be prepared for us at the university, but the students still had to travel outside of Lagos for our work assignment. We were there to furnish the labor for the building of a maternity ward.

Our local sponsor was a very proper Mrs. S. She was visiting me one afternoon when Jonathan, one of the students, came out of the shower with a towel wrapped around him and a few minutes later, Beverly, a female student, descended from that same shower room – also wrapped in a towel. Mrs. S. came close to fainting and told me, with a great deal of controlled anger, that "this is highly improper". I assured her that the showers had private stalls. That did not satisfy her. She wanted me to move the female students to another compound. I said that I would not, and she said: "I shall tell the authorities". I told her that I was the authority. She said that she would call the American Ambassador, which she promptly did. The ambassador's wife called me, and I explained that the students did not want, nor did they need, to be separated and that I would not change my mind. She asked: "Suppose the ambassador told you to do so?". I said: "Such an order would be beyond his jurisdiction. He did not pay for us to come here and he cannot supervise our arrangements". She said: "Well, I tried" and left it like that. However, that would not end my contact with the embassy. (Today, Jonathan is the renowned Rev. Jonathan Weaver, pastor of one of the biggest churches in Upper Marlboro, Md.)

The students were finding it very difficult to adjust to the Nigerian cuisine – which consisted of one-part meat and an equal part hot pepper, the kind that even Mexicans and Jamaicans might hesitate to eat. I noticed that the students were beginning to lose weight and I got a little scared. I called the American Embassy and the ambassador's wife answered the phone. Without much of a preamble, I asked her if she would give us a party. Her response: "Is this the same Professor Raiford who told me to mind my own business"? I replied: "Not really the same one. This one is eating humble pie. Will you please give us a party?" She asked when I wanted the party and I told her that she should give it that same night and to make sure that there would be lots of food. I also said that she should send some cars to transport us. The embassy was very accommodating. The embassy staff also invited us to their 4th of July picnic. As for the food situation, in time, the students made the adjustment and began to actually enjoy the cuisine.

I was assigned a car and a driver to take me to and from City Hall where I held my classes. I taught Social Case Work in the morning and Advanced Public Administration in the afternoon. I taught the same content and methods that accredited graduate schools teach in the country. I learned that human beings are considerably alike and hardly different at all, geography notwithstanding.

I shall always be grateful to the University of Kansas for helping to make my trip to Africa possible. Nevertheless, Lawrence, Kansas could never be my home. After two years in the boondocks, I was ready for Chicago.

10: FROM ZUBER TO CHICAGO

Unless you are fond of the prairie and tumbleweeds, two years in Kansas are quite enough! So, when an invitation came in the form of recruitment into a doctoral program at the University of Chicago, my bags were almost nearly packed. Although this meant that we would be leaving the beautiful house we had designed and built and uprooting the children from a stellar public school, we were all ready for the new horizon.

We did not know anyone in Chicago, but it did not take long for that to change. Our first newly made friends were Dr. Leon Chestang and his wife Aurelia. Leon was on the faculty of the School of Social Service Administration at the University of Chicago and had taken it upon himself to serve as the "welcome committee" for the few African American students who were entering the doctoral program. Within a week of our arrival, the Chestangs invited us to dinner and extended a friendship that would endure. Our second set of friends was Dr. William and Merrietta Pollard. Bill was in his second year of doctoral study and Merrietta was studying for her MSW. They were a stunning young couple. Bill's boyish looks masked a serious scholar who was destined to go far in the social work and higher education arenas. The Pollards, recognizing that I was a full-time student with three small children, understood that I might need a respite from time to time and graciously gave me the key to their apartment in Hyde Park to use when they were out-of-town. The third friend would not come to Chicago for another year. She was Dr. Mary Davidson. She came to the University of Chicago as an administrator. She had already attained her doctorate. Mary, Bill, Chestang, and I became lifelong friends and all three played a very important role in my professional development: Bill became dean of a nascent school of social work at Grambling University and recruited me there to help conceptualize a focus for the program. (Later, Bill would go on to become the Dean of the School of Social Work at Syracuse University as well as the president of the University of the District of Columbia.) Leon, as Dean of the School of Social Work at Wayne State University, awarded me the Martin Luther King/Rosa Parks Chair. (For a semester, I taught in Miami the first half of the week and in Detroit the second half.) Mary became dean of the School of Social Work at the University of Illinois and later, the Dean at Rutgers State University School of Social Work. As Dean, Mary gave me several lucrative consulting assignments, but she did considerably more, and I will tell you about that later. Also, so convinced was Mary that I could write (even more convinced than I was) that when she was asked to write a review of a nationally published textbook, she handed the assignment to me. I wrote the review for which I was given quite a liberal stipend.

As for the School of Social Service Administration, I was a misfit from the very beginning. Helen Harris Perlman, perhaps the best-known social work educator at that time, and considered the queen of casework, was one of my professors. To demonstrate social pathology, she selected only African American cases. Every case used to study the dynamics of unwed motherhood was of an African American. The same was true when talking about poverty, crime, and dysfunctional families. When I challenged her on this tendency, she pulled out her statistics that showed a greater percentage of African Americans vs white Americans were in these categories. I was not fooled by the percentages and did my own research and brought to class evidence to show that the greater number of people in these frowned upon categories were white not African American and I wanted to know why she could not find even one such case to present to the class. Also, I challenged her on her selection of pioneers of social work because she named only white people – with a great deal of emphasis on Jane Addams and Florence Kelley. I reminded her of the contributions made by such African Americans as Mary Church Terrell and Ida B. Wells. Needless to say, I was not her prize student! However, that was just the beginning. I refused to buy into the philosophy of the School regarding social welfare policy. The focus was on "the greatest amount of good for the greatest number of people", meaning that society would do alright if there were just a few expendable people. I did not, and cannot, see any single person as expendable. I expressed my preference that social welfare policy should guarantee "the greatest amount of good" to all people and insisted that the only way to eradicate, or even reduce poverty and crime was to accept this particular premise. I was not popular with these professors either. I was even more dismayed by the economic philosophy of Milton Friedman who taught that a certain level of unemployment was acceptable and helped the Reagan Administration to conceptualize the "trickledown effect" and to create economic policies that have led to the crisis that we are in today. (Ten years later, it was my pleasure to take a course from Paul Samuelson at the Kennedy School at Harvard whose economic theory was just the opposite of Friedman's.) With all my ranting and raving, there was no way the University of Chicago was going to award me a PhD. The claim was that I could neither conceptualize or write and, therefore, would not be allowed to enter the dissertation phase of the PhD program. (I was amused by the comment made by the President of the National Association of Black Social Workers, Cenie Williams: "To say that Gil cannot write is the same as saying that Shakespeare could not write", an over the top compliment of course.

Fortunately for me, Chicago was more than the university. I met other lifelong friends in the community. Among them were Jerry, Hank, Henry J., Brenda, Rudy, and Mary. We played pinochle practically every weekend. Also, Jerry and Hank gave me keys to their apartment so that I would have a quiet place to go and study while they were at work. Also, fortunately for me, the University of Chicago did not have a monopoly on PhD programs. Even so, I had practically given up on ever attainting a doctorate. However, Dr. Mary Davidson had not given up on me. She insisted that I apply for admission to the program at Brandeis, her own Alma Mater. For a long time, I demurred, but Mary was persistent – even going so far as to put me in touch with a good friend of hers who was on the faculty at Brandeis, who turned out to be a Gomer Pyle speaking white man from Alabama, and one the most genuine persons I had ever met. He was also on the Admissions Committee and was on the look-out for my application package, which turned out to be a decided blessing: In sending my transcript to Brandeis, someone from the University of Chicago had placed a letter in the packet advising against my acceptance – claiming that I was too radical and would be too disruptive. Dr. Wyatt Jones intercepted the letter and destroyed it meaning that the committee never got to see that letter and I was duly admitted.

One last commentary on the University of Chicago: Yet another serendipitous incident. Although Dr. Chestang was already a very popular professor at the University of Chicago and Dr. Davidson was a renowned administrator, with a fantastic record as a fund-raiser, the faculty refused to grant tenure to either of these phenomenal educators, which turned out to be a blessing in disguise. Dr. Davidson left Chicago and went to Southern Illinois where she established a School of Social Work and installed herself as dean. Eventually, she left there to become dean of the School of Social work at Rutgers University. As for Dr. Chestang, a prolific author of publications dealing with race and cultural issues, he became dean of other prestigious Schools of Social Work. Dr. Pollard Established a Department of Social Work at Grambling University and went on to become a dean of social work at a prestigious university and even a university president. My relationship with these three professionals persisted through the years; Dr. Davidson gave me consultation employment; Dr. Chestang awarded me the Martin Luther King/Rosa Parks Chair at Wayne State University; and Dr. Pollard hired me to come to

Grambling to help in the founding of that school's Department of Social Work.

Although I had successfully completed all the course work for a doctorate at the University of Chicago, Brandeis insisted that I would have to take all of the courses that were offered in their program. I was working at Barry University at that time but was able to get a two-year educational leave of absence. I completed the course work in a year and a half; wrote my area paper the next week, my dissertation the week after that, and defended the following week. This meant that I had another six months before I needed to return to Barry. I used that time to go and teach in Japan and Okinawa.

11: TEACHING IN THE MILITARY

As you already know, I refused to sign up to be drafted and I refused to take the obligatory ROTC that was required of all Hampton male freshmen. Yet, I was never anti-military and was, in fact, an avid letter writer to all my friends and relatives who were in the service. Nevertheless, it is ironic that my most challenging and edifying teaching experience was as a professor teaching on military bases.

I do not know how it happened but one day toward the end of the 1970's, I received a call from a dean at Pepperdine University asking if I would be willing to teach classes on military bases. The students would be mostly officers seeking a graduate degree. I would teach four hours on Friday nights, all day on Saturdays, and a half-day on Sunday – every other weekend. I would be provided a plane ticket, a car rental voucher, hotel accommodations, and a liberal per diem. Also, the salary was decent.

It did not take me long to figure out that I would mainly be teaching white males, many of them would be older than I, and *all* of them would be endowed with a sense of superiority. I knew I would have to deal with that superficial issue before any teaching or learning could take place. By this time, I had been in enough universities by administered white people to know that only white males don't have to prove their competence. They are presumed to be competent until they are proven otherwise. All others must prove their competence from the outset. I intended to do just that:

With every new group of students I taught, I began the lecture by talking way over their heads and did not stop until I was sure that I had gotten their full attention. Then, I would go back and begin to teach. At Hampton, I had learned pedagogy, meaning that I could successfully teach young learners – including typical university students. However, these officers were no ordinary students, but serious adult learners, looking to challenge me whenever possible. I silently gave thanks to the Lord for directing me to get a degree in androgyny! My first master's at New York University was in Higher Education. Whereas younger students are grade-oriented, these officers would be utility –oriented, meaning that *all* the content had to be meaningful as well as an addition to what they already knew or thought they knew. With this understanding, I promised my classes that if at any session anyone felt that he (and sometimes she) did not learn something new, I would ask the university to refund the money that was paid for that particular course.

Aside from the actual process of teaching, two paradigms serve as my guide to education: I firmly believe that all learning is conceptual. (I did not always believe this but two incidents convinced me that it is so. The first one occurred when Aunt Sadie sent her high school grandchild to me to help her with the "new math". I had absolutely no idea what any of that stuff was. However, I read the introduction in the front of the textbook and the introduction to all the chapters. There was no way I would even attempt to do the operations, but I could tell Cynthia what it was that she must do. Once she understood the concept, she was able to breeze through the assignment. The other incident had to do with a Japanese doctoral student studying astrophysics. He paid me well to tutor him for a final exam. Now, I have not taken a science class since biology 101 at Hampton – which I barely passed. Again, I spent a few hours reading what it was that the student was expected to learn.

Out of a class of 45, that student received the third highest grade on the exam.)

My other belief is that everyone who is not brain damaged or otherwise mentally/emotionally disabled has the capacity to learn everything that anyone else can learn – but not the same way and not with the same rate of speed. It is incumbent upon a teacher to ascertain the learning style of students and not to assume that "one size fits all".

So, by the time I began my career as an itinerant military professor, I was quite confident that I could teach these officers, their presumed high-quality undergraduate education notwithstanding. In the military, I taught many courses that I had taught before on college campuses, but I doubled the content as well as the speed. These officers were a joy to teach – mainly because their very presence forced me to prepare well before each class.

I only had one near negative incident. It happened, or could have happened, at Kadena Air Force base in Okinawa. It was my method to give a very rigorous objective mid-term examination. It was designed to test just how well the students understood and contextualized the content. Any student who correctly answered all 50 items would be exempt from having to take the final. Up to this time, I had had no African America to qualify for an exemption. In no class did I tell the students in advance about this policy and would tell the exempted student only at the end of the last lecture. At Kadena, this student was the lone exemption and the lone African American in the class. When I told him that he was exempted from taking the final and told him why, he was mollified! He advised me that I could not do that. He said no matter how I would try to explain or justify exempting him, it would be viewed as racial favoritism. I told him that my policy stands and that they, meaning the white students, could cry and complain until the end of time. The Black student was adamant and insisted that he would take the exam anyway. I said that he could, but that I would not grade or read his essays. He did and I didn't.

Teaching on military bases in foreign countries seemed to have required the professor to have a military rank. I was made an honorary colonel, a rank I probably would never have attained if I were actually in the military. To tell the truth, I could get used to being a colonel! Not only was I given a furnished house and a housekeeper, all my overseas flights were in first class on military aircraft – with three stewards. Although, I was often the lone first-class passenger.

During the six years I taught in the military, I taught 23 different courses. Although I taught in every branch, I was partial to the Air Force. This is where I found the most challenging students.

Also, during those six years, I was still working full-time at Barry University and working part-time with the U. S. Department of State. You must wonder why I was working so much: First of all, none of it seemed like real work because I was never tired or stressed out. However, just as importantly, I actually needed the money. At various times during this period, my two daughters were at Brown University in Rhode Island; one son was in a boarding school at Interlochen Arts Academy in Michigan; and my other son was studying in Language Villages in Minnesota. The occurrence of my next noteworthy adventure remains a mystery to me and must remain a mystery for you until the next segment.

12: FROM ZUBER TO WASHINGTON DC

When I realized that I would have a career in higher education, which comes with free summers and extended holiday seasons, including Spring Breaks, I decided to go to DC and seek part-time employment with the U.S. Government. My first and only stop was at the Department of State. I explained that I was looking for a part-time job that involved travel and/or working with foreigners. Lucky for me, such a job existed. Because I had traveled extensively and had, in fact, visited many foreign countries. It also helped that I still had some knowledge of French. I had no trouble passing the exam and was given a perennial contract, which is still in effect. I was hired as an Escort/Interpreter, one of six who had that job at the time,

For someone who wants to know everything and everybody, the Escort/Interpreting job was a sociological smorgasbord. Usually, I would get anywhere from a couple of weeks to a couple of months advanced notice of an assignment and I would waste no time preparing for it. In that space of time, I would learn all I could about the various professions of the incoming visitors. I would learn the vocabulary as well as the salient issues so that when I sat in on professional meetings, I could follow the discussions. I would learn about the visitors' respective countries, including their political systems, their cultures, and their literature – knowing that fiction is sometimes the most authentic revelation of a people.

Through the years, the profession that interested me the most was the one dealing with justice. I would say that some of my most interesting assignments included working with judges and lawyers. However, my first experience with judges was not a particularly pleasant one. The visitors were eight Supreme Court judges from a West African country. This was during the time *before* there was airport "security" and we could actually meet the visitors as they deplaned. These particular visitors had not seen, or had chosen to ignore, the sign I was holding that identified me as their American host. I saw eight elaborately dressed men standing in a corner in deep conversation and there were many bags still going around on the moving belt. I assumed that these men had to be the visitors and went to interrupt them to confirm. They were the visitors and those were their bags, but they made no move to retrieve them. Instead, they asked: "Where are the boys"? Honestly, I had no idea what they meant but they immediately clarified this for me: "The boys to carry our bags. Doesn't the U.S. know that we are Supreme Court Judges and cannot carry bags?" I told them that they did not have to carry their many bags – that we have an industry here called "porterage" and that I could arrange for them not to ever have to carry a bag throughout their stay here, but each would have to give me $200 in advance to pay for this service and that I would return to them any unused money, but that I might ask them for more if this amount proved not to be sufficient. That was settled but it was only the beginning.

Their arrival was on a Saturday. Our first professional appointment was scheduled for 8:30 a.m. the following Monday. I received a call from one of them at 6:30 a.m., advising me that I must cancel the appointment because they were "indisposed". I wanted to know in what way they were indisposed. He explained to me that they were entertained by their ambassador during the night and did not get their full complement of sleep. As tactfully as I could manage at 6:30 in the morning, I advised him that the

U.S. Supreme Court is one third of the U.S. government and that they should not expect to remain here as our guests if they, in fact, snubbed our government. I said that I fully expected to see them all at breakfast at 7:30 so that we would have ample time to get to our appointment. They were there, but that was just episode two.

Two days before we were to leave Washington, I gave them their airline tickets to the several cities that we were to visit. They were appalled, exclaiming; "These are not first-class tickets!" I explained to them that we are not an aristocracy and cannot use taxpayer money to create class differentiation. They were adamant and insisted that they must travel first class. I told them that I could upgrade their tickets to first class but that they would have to pay the difference – which would be considerable. They would pay it. I explained further (making this up as things were developing) that they would also have to upgrade my ticket because the State Department would not want me to travel in a class less than that of the visitors. Done. However, that was not the final round: They insisted that I locate and reserve dinner for them at *the best* restaurants in every city we were to visit. I said that I would, but that I would not be able to dine with them because my per diem did not accommodate "fine dining". They said that I would be their dinner guest and, of course, there was no objection!

The final round came when we were leaving San Francisco for NYC. American Airlines had the nerve to bump us out of first class – however graciously. The airline offered to fly us to NYC in tourist class free and return all the monies that had been paid for first class tickets. A check would be sent to each of us within a week. That was not satisfactory, causing me to forget that I was a public diplomat and returning me to my Zuber roots! Without a great deal of tack, I reminded them that both classes arrive at the same time and that it would be foolish to wait for a later flight and squander a day that could be spent in the most exciting city in the world. They relented but asked the airline to make one check and send it to me. I told them that I would buy international money orders and send each person an equal share. I did as they requested, but imagine my surprise when each of them signed the money orders over to me and sent them back!

The experience with these judges was an anomaly. I could pretty much count on having a great experience with judges and lawyers and got to meet several interesting people I would not have met otherwise. These included Sandra Day O'Conner who told me that she was a mentor to Cecil Patterson, a very good friend of mine from Hampton and also a Superior court judge in Arizona at that time; Judge Lance Ito, of the O.J. murder case; and Timothy McVeigh, the man who bombed the Oklahoma Federal Courthouse (I accompanied a judge who wanted to interview McVeigh who was on death row in a prison in Colorado). Also, I accompanied a group of Ghanaian judges who went to Chicago to visit with a panel of federal appellate court judges, one of whom took us with her for a Sunday church service where we met Rev. Wright who was still in Mr. Obama's good graces at the time.

Through the years, I escorted attorneys who visited from every region in the world and who met with lawyers in large firms and deans of law schools. These meetings helped me to become practically proficient in constitutional law. However, my favorite of all the legal specialties was/is Intellectual Property Law.

Although I have mentioned only judges and lawyers, they were only one of the many types of professionals that I got to know: there were teachers, farmers, gold miners, university professors, athletes, medical doctors, artists, scientists, parliamentarians, mayors, military generals, and more. Of all the various jobs that I have held, this one was the most educationally and emotionally rewarding,

13: FROM THE COMPANY QUARTERS OF ZUBER TO BUCKINGHAM PALACE IN LONDON

No, I did not stay in Buckingham Palace. In fact, I have never even been inside the palace, However, I rode past it nearly every day for about a month. This chapter is about how that came to be:

In January 1992, I received a strange telephone call from a man who identified himself as the Consul General for the British government. He wanted to know if I would accept an invitation from "Her Majesty's Government" to visit the United Kingdom. I simply laughed and asked if this was some kind of joke. His reply, a very sober reply: "Her Majesty's Government never jokes!" I said that I would be delighted to visit England as a guest, and I wanted to know what would be required of me. He advised me that only two things would be required: (1) I would have to submit to them a list containing all the places I wanted to visit and all the people that I wanted to meet who are engaged in my profession of social services. And (2) I needed to give them the date on which I wanted to begin the visit. (It never entered my wooly head to ask them why I was being invited in the first place – and to this day, I still do not know why.)

I was teaching full-time at Barry University, but I decided that I could reasonably go during Spring Break and requested and received permission to be absent for two weeks beyond the spring break vacation. I was sent a first-class ticket to fly on British Air and I was on my way – somewhat giddy and filled with barely contained curiosity. When the plane landed at Heathrow, an agent from the Home Office (the counterpart of our State Department) boarded the plane to escort me off. He asked for my baggage claim checks and said that my luggage would be delivered to "your car." I was just about to tell him that I definitely would not risk driving in London because I would likely forget that I was supposed to drive on the wrong side of the street, when he quickly informed me that "your driver is called Wally". He then introduced me to a young lady who he called Baroness somebody and said that she would be my London based escort/guide and when I would travel beyond that city, I would be assigned someone else. Wally drove the Baroness and me to a five-star hotel located near Buckingham Palace. There, the Baroness gave me a printed copy of my itinerary, a government credit card, and some train tickets I would use to visit Liverpool, Stratford-on-the-Avon, and Oxford – the places that I had said I wanted to visit. At the hotel, I was given a penthouse suite with a very large living room replete with a large bowl of fresh fruit and several large bouquets of freshly cut flowers and I began to think of the song "for all we know, this might only be a dream". I also allowed myself a spark of vanity and kept thinking:" If my friends could see me now! "

I began my myriad of meetings the next day. The first meeting was a teleconference with an assortment of agency heads that explained the types of services each provided. I was very impressed by the Department of Corrections. I was informed that inmates whose jail time is a year or less would be able to return to their apartments because the government will have paid their monthly rents thereby reducing the incidence of homelessness. I was also impressed by the health system which assigns social workers to new mothers who would visit them right after the birth of a child in order to make a determination about the family's unmet needs. The social worker would also visit the home about a month after the mother and child were discharged in order to evaluate the condition of the habitat. Even my escort, the Baroness, had a social worker with whom she met on a monthly basis to insure the well-being of the child and family. I think my greatest surprise came when I visited a group home of six elderly Black men in Liverpool. Each had his own large private room and they shared a common room, a cook, and a housekeeper. They were given a pension, the equivalent of about $50 per week. The social worker explained to me that this was not enough money and that she was fighting to get them a raise. I wanted to know how much they were paying for their keep and was advised that each man paid $35 per week. I said that it seemed to me that they had quite enough income. She said: "No, what about their vacation!" I reminded her that they are retired – on a permanent vacation. She explained that everyone should be able to close down everything and go to the seaside for a month each year and enjoy being served and enjoy being free from work and worry. (I thought of the two weeks' vacation hardworking people in the U.S. are begrudgingly given and I silently cringed.)

Being a guest of the government automatically bestows on one the V.I.P. status, a status with which I am most uncomfortable. I had not realized just how uncomfortable until the day I was to be the guest of honor at a banquet at a predominately black township of Brixton. When we arrived at city hall, many elegantly dressed people were waiting in the front of the building to greet me. I just could not see myself descending from a chauffeur-driven Rolls Royce and waiting for a white driver to open the door for me. I asked Wally to drive around the corner and that I would walk back. I insisted over his vehement protest.

My program included a visit to the House of Parliament where I was to meet with the two Black Parliamentarians, Bernie Grant, and Paul Boateng, and the House of Lords, where I was to meet with Lord David Pitt, the lone Black in the House of Lords. At first, Bernie was prepared to let me know that the Blacks in England did not need African Americans to come to that country to teach them anything. When I convinced him that I was there to learn and not teach, he was much more cordial, and we had a great meeting. Paul, despite my efforts to be friendly, remained officious. I knew that he had been slated for an important ministerial position and I dared to ask him if he carried the Black agenda. He said that he carried the agenda of his constituents who were mostly white, and he added: "I am only half black". Before I could hold it in check, the Zuber in me came out and I told him, in the most emphatic way I would muster, that even though he might be a delight to his white mother, the whole world sees him and identifies him as a black man – not a half black man! I explained that his blackness is an albatross and that he will never be able to shed it. As you can imagine, that exchange did not sit well with him. As for Lord David Pitt, he was simply delightful. He took the time to give me a personal tour around the House of Lords. (Paul Boateng eventually became the British High Commissioner to South Africa. Lord Pitt was ailing at the time of my visit and would live only two more years.)

My most interesting episode during this visit was at an event that challenged my lackadaisical attitude toward cosmic mystery: I was invited to an affair in

Merton, another black township. I had not realized that I was to be the guest of honor and, therefore, expected to make an after-dinner speech. I had prepared nothing, and I told that to the audience before beginning to make a speech – a speech which, to this day, I cannot recall. What I do recall is that I was given a standing ovation. Many people came up to greet me, but I can remember only two – a husband and wife who introduced themselves as Mr. and Mrs. Semple. They said to me, regarding my lack of preparation to make a speech: "Dr. Raiford, you really do not have to worry. You have a Guardian Angel who steps in when you need help." They went on to say that everyone has such an Angel, but that those Angels are not equally vigilant. Their statement caused me to revisit many unexplained events in my life, including this invitation tendered by the British government. I also began to remember how, being on welfare, I was able to attend and graduate from an expensive preparatory school. I remember my first Christmas in Miami when I had only $14 and wondered how I would provide Christmas presents for my family and how I took that $14 to the Dog Tracks and was instructed on how to bet and won

$600. I also remember another Christmas when I began receiving expensive jewelry in the mail from an unknown benefactor. (The "gifts" kept coming until I refused any more packages. I took all the items to Service Merchandise, the store from which they came – explaining that I did not order any of those things. I was told that they had already been purchased but the store refused to tell me who purchased them. Still thinking that it was a mistake, I stashed everything in a closet for one year and when it seemed that no one was coming to reclaim them, I took everything back to Service Merchandise and was given the cash – enough money to take my entire immediate family to San Francisco for a weeklong vacation.) I was the beneficiary of several other unexplained "gifts" and opportunities. When there are no natural explanations, I think it is not entirely fickle to accept a supernatural explanation – to wit, I do believe that I have a very vigilant Guardian Angel, for which I am unequivocally grateful. (Maybe I did something good in another life.)

On my last day in London, the Home Office gave me a luncheon. The officials wanted to know my assessment of race relations in England. I praised them for their very progressive social service programs, but I told them that it was my impression that the Blacks in England do not "feel" British and that they are not fully integrated into the national fabric of that country. At that time, I saw no Black newscasters, no Blacks in television commercials, and very few Blacks representing England in international competitions, etc. They told me that that would change and, as I write this, I believe it is beginning to do so.

THE EPILOGUE
Famous People I have known

Growing up in Zuber, my dreams were kept quite modest. Maybe that was because when you are poor and black and the product of a loving, but struggling family, there is no vista. So, I was incredibly surprised when my classmates at that prestigious academy voted me the most ambitious student among them. I was taken aback. Then, and never, have I thought of myself as ambitious. I have always just been me, the wandering son of an unschooled mother who happened to have been the most brilliant person that I have ever known. She was quite a savant in preparing me to meet life head on, without getting "big-headed" myself. When I look back over my life, I recall meeting and interacting with many world-famous people, people who could not tell that I am a plain ole country boy! The following is a list of those who I can recall:

Zara Gully: You should remember Ms. Gully. She is the actress who played the feisty mother of George Jefferson in "The Jefferson's". Ms. Gully taught me acting when I was a student at Fessenden.

John McClendon: Coach McClendon is in the Basketball Hall of Fame. He was one of the first basketball players to play the game. He was taught the game by James Naismith, the inventor of basketball. John was the only black student among the original players, and he went on to become world famous. He coached me both at Fessenden and briefly at Hampton.

Eddie Robinson: He is famous for winning more football games than any coach in history, including the legendary Don Shula. We had lunch together practically every day during the sabbatical year that I spent at Grambling University. Barry University, where I was a professor, proffered him an honorary doctorate. Coach Robinson was an extremely modest, as well as private man. He declined to accept the honor.

John Riggins: John was a famous NFL player and the MVP in several high schools, universities, and NFL tournaments. He was one of my students when I taught at the University of Kansas.

Evander Holyfield: I sat next to the boxing champion on a flight from New Orleans to Miami and had a very nice conversation all the way.

Muhammed Ali: I met Mr. Ali when my son, Douglas, was about three years old and we were returning from a speaking engagement that I had in NYC. We were changing planes in Norfolk at the time when he put Douglas on his shoulder and walked around the boarding area.

Doug Williams: I met Mr. Williams when we were leaving the baggage claim area at Miami National Airport. He had come to meet Don Shula and was about to hail a cab when I offered to give him a lift into town. We spent the entire ride talking about his legendary college football college coach, and my Grambling lunch buddy, Eddie Robinson. History will remember Doug as the first African American quarterback to win a Superbowl as well as being named the Most Valuable Player.

Mrs. Armstrong: She was the widow of **General Armstrong,** the titular founder of Hampton Institute. Mrs. Armstrong was 20 years old when she came to teach at Hampton. The General was already an old man. He married her and she survived him by many years. After he died, she established a residential family camp in New Hampshire. As a student at Hampton, I went to work for her during the summer recesses for three years. (The camp was established in 1885 and has continued to operate until now).

Mrs. Maria Phenix: Mrs. Phenix was the widow of George Phenix, next to the last white president of Hampton. The Phenix High school is named after him. When I found that I could not complete my studies at Hampton because of financial reasons, Mrs. Phenix gave me a room and bathroom in her own home, paid for my meal tickets and gave me an allowance of $10 per week for my last two years at Hampton. Her only son, Paul Phenix, was an ambassador to Portugal and later, a judge at the Nuremberg trials of the Nazis in Germany.

Ms. Marian Anderson: When Ms. Anderson came to Hampton to give a concert, she could not stay at the local hotels. She accepted Mrs. Phenix's invitation to spend two nights with us. Years later, I escorted Ms. Anderson to W.C. Handy's funeral (Mr. Handy is historically known as the Father of the Blues) in New York. The line of people wanting to get into the church stretched several blocks. When Mrs. Anderson arrived in her chauffeur driven limo, I noticed that she was alone. I helped her out of the car and escorted into the church. We had front row seats.

Ms. Ruth Brown: Ms. Brown lived in the same building as Uncle Julius and Aunt Sadie, I lived with them for several months. **Frankie Lyman,** of the famous Teenagers singing group, also lived in that building.

Ms. Gladys Knight: I met Ms. Knight about a month after she was married to the radio personality and Inspirational Speaker, **Les Brown**, who I had met years earlier when he came to speak to my class at Barry. Gladys and I had breakfast together when we were both guests at a Sheraton Hotel.

Richard Pryor: During the winter of 1960, Mr. Pryor and I co-taught a course for Ethical Culture in New York City. Richard had just gotten out of the army where he had served two years. He was discharged for fighting with a white soldier because of the soldier's racist remarks.

Redd Foxx: I met Mr. John Sanford during my first trip to Las Vegas. Both of us seemed to have been addicted to the Keno game, so much so that after everyone else had given up and gone to bed, we were the lone players – both losing but I enjoyed talking with him about his Sanford and Son show.

Thelonious Monk: Mr. Monk, the famous jazz musician, was a fixture at the Five Spot, a small jazz establishment located less than a block from where I lived in East Greenwich Village. Many days, I would be waiting for him in front of the Five Spot when Baroness Rothchild would drive him there. He would allow me to sit in on his rehearsals.

John Coltrane: John was a world-famous saxophonist. He lived in my building in the East Village. Coltrane had just moved from Philadelphia to the East Village when I met him. He came to New York so that he could work with Monk and Miles Davis. They made Jazz history at that little hole-in-the-wall bar, The Five Spot.

Lionel Hampton: When Lionel came to perform in Miami, we took our son, Lance, to meet him. He was glad to know that Lance was interested in playing the vibraphone. He showed Lance a few moves and allowed Lance to play on that famous vibraphone.

Ms. Maria Callas: Ms. Callas was a world-famous opera diva. She would often rehearse at the Amato Opera House in the East Village and I would often go to hear her sing. She would often allow me to sit in on her rehearsals. I was able to see the operas without paying a great deal of money by having to go to the Met.

Ms. Vinnette Carroll: Vinnette was a famous Broadway actress and a noted playwright whose best-known works are "Don't Bother Me, I Can't Cope" and "Your Arms are too Short to Box with God". When she relocated from NYC to south Florida, we invited her to our house for dinner. She came, and we had a great time.

Philip Michael Thomas: I first met Michael when he was starring in Miami Vice. However, I really did not get to know him until later. He purchased a theater building in North Miami near my home. I often visited him there. At that time, he was a vegetarian and he taught me how to select delectable dishes when we would meet at a local restaurant.

The Wayans family: We lived in the same housing complex with this family when the kids were very young. One night, NYC lost electric power and there was no light anywhere. I remember that the young Wayans brothers had lighted candles and took turns walking residents up those dark stairways. We lived on the 18th floor. I shall always be grateful to them for that.

Whoopi Goldberg lived in that same complex, but I did not know her. She was just a toddler then. Her mother was employed in the daycare center that was in that complex.

Dr. Margaret Walker: Dr. Walker is famous for her epic poem "For My People" and for the best-selling historical novel, Jubilee. I went to Jackson, Mississippi. looking for her and found her on the campus of Jackson State University. I took her to lunch and later she and I were invited to participate in the graduation ceremony at Jackson State and I got to walk with her in the procession.

Ernest Gaines: Mr. Gaines is most famous for his novels The Autobiography of Miss Jane Pittman and A Lesson before Dying. I met Mr. Gaines when he and his wife, Dianne (nee) Smith, lived in Miami. Dianne was the incomparable New Year's Eve party giver and my family was always invited to her parties, which never failed to be a hit with the elite of Miami (don't know how we were snuck into that group)!

Ms. Anne Rice: Ms. Rice is best known as the queen of vampire novels. I went to visit her in her home on St. Charles Street in New Orleans. I was provided home hospitality. She lived in a huge haunted looking mansion. She eventually sold it and moved around the corner from St. Charles.

Ms Margaret Mead: Ms. Mead was a world-famous anthropologist. She would often give free lectures at Cooper Union in the East Village. I attended all of them and would often walk her to the subway. When she became curator at the Museum of History, she invited me to have lunch with her and **Ruth Benedict**, another famous anthropologist.

Andy Shallal: Mr. Shallal is the founder and CEO of the thematic restaurant, "Busboys and Poets", which memorializes the life of the African American poet, Langston Hughes. He is a strong advocate for peace and universal brother/sisterhood. Ralph Nader has dubbed Mr. Shallal," Democracy's Restaurateur."

Barbara Jordan: Ms. Jordan was the first African American elected to the state senate in Texas and the first southern African American woman to be elected to the U.S. House of Representatives. I met her when she was a professor of Law School at the U. of Texas in Austin. I had taken a group of international parliamentarians to the University of Texas who wanted to dialogue with her.

Dr. James Dumpson: Dr. Dumpson was the Commissioner of Welfare when I was an employee in that agency. When I protested having to punch a clock in order to prove my attendance at work, I was not fired, However, I was called downtown to meet with the Commissioner. We discussed other positions in the agency that did not have that requirement and he allowed me to select from among those. That is how I got to be the official representative of the department of Welfare in Family Court.

Ms. Helen Harris Perlman: Ms. Perlman wrote the textbook that ALL of the schools of social work used to introduce students to the profession. She was one of my professors when I was a student at the University of Chicago. Ms. Perlman was a leading pioneer in social work education and was often referred to as The Queen of Social Work.

Dr. John Hope Franklin: Dr. Franklin was considered the most renowned historian of African American History. He was one of my professors at the University of Chicago. I last saw Dr. Franklin when we had lunch together at the Zora Neal Hurston festival in Eatonville, Florida in 2007. He was one of the main speakers at that event and the 92-year-old man lectured for an hour without a single written note.

Dr. Roland Warren: Dr. Warren pioneered Community Organization education as a method of social work. He was the author of the bestselling textbook used in practically every school of social work to teach Community Organization. He was one of my professors at Brandeis University. I used his book when I taught the course.

Milton Friedman: He is best known for creating the concept of Reagannomics. President Reagan used that concept to justify reducing taxes on the rich. Friedman thought that by enabling the super-rich to retain more of their money, that cohort would be more likely to give to the poor and he called that "The trickle-down effect." He had not reasoned that the super-rich are also super stingy and would not give any of that windfall to the poor. I was in his class at the U. of Chicago and argued vehemently with him during every class period.

Dick Gregory: Mr. Gregory hired me to tutor his daughter, Pamela, when they lived in the Hyde Park area of Chicago and she was in the 6th grade. The tutoring was done in their home, meaning that I got to meet the entire family.

Alvin Ailey: Alvin was just starting out on his way to fame. He was quite slender when I first met him. He was in a dance group that often performed at Cooper Union. He would occasionally stop by my apartment, with several of the other dancers, for refreshments. The last time I saw Alvin in-person, he had organized his own dance company and was performing in Stockholm, Sweden. He gave me free tickets to the performance.

James Baldwin: I met James when we arrived at the same time at the American Express Office in Paris to collect our mail. I had a copy of his latest novel with me and he saw it and was delighted to know that I had purchased a copy and was reading it. He told me that he was just passing through Paris on his way to Marrakesh, Morocco where he was planning an international party and he invited me to attend. I couldn't because I had already enrolled in the Sorbonne University. Besides, I did not think that this Zuber boy was ready to hang with the big boys!

A Philip Randolph: Mr. Randolph gained his fame by organizing the Brotherhood of Sleeping Car Porters, the first national labor union for Blacks in this country. He also organized the first march on Washington designed to force the integration of the military. The President capitulated and the march was called off. However, he joined Martin Luther King with the 1963 March on Washington. In fact, he was among the first speakers. I first met Mr. Randolph when he came to speak to us at Fessenden and met him years later when he permitted me to spend a month with him to write one of my master's theses, using him as my subject.

Mrs. Eleanor Roosevelt: I met Mrs. Roosevelt at one of her birthday parties. I was working at the Wiltwyck School for Boys and she was on the Board. She invited me and my eight charges to the party. Years later, when one of the boys had become a vicious teenager and committed murder and was given the death sentence, I contacted Mrs. Roosevelt and asked if she would join me in trying to get his sentence changed to life in prison rather than the electric chair. We prevailed.

James Robinson: Mr. Robinson is famous for establishing Operation Crossroads Africa, the organization that inspired the creation of the U.S. Peace Corps. Mr. Robinson selected me to teach social work and public administration to government officials in Lagos, Nigeria. (It was such an honor because I was among the 20 people, out of 200 applicants, selected to go to Africa that summer.)

Judge Jane Bolin: Judge Bolin is thought to have been the first Black female judge in the country. She was a judge in family court in NYC. I was the court representative for the NYC Dept. of Welfare, and I appeared before her several times.

Judge Randolph Baxter: I met Judge Randolph Baxter when I escorted a group of African Supreme Court judges to meet with him, and several other times when I visited Cleveland, Ohio. Judge Baxter is famous because of his status as being the first African American to be appointed to the bench in the U.S. Bankruptcy Court.

Supreme Court Justice, Sandra Day O'Connor: I had lunch with the judge when I was escorting the only female Supreme Court Judge of Somalia around the country for the U.S. Dept. of State. On this same tour, I had lunch with **Lance Ito,** the judge in the O. J. Simpson case. Also, on this same trip, I met with **James McVeigh** on death row, where he was awaiting execution for killing nearly 200 and injuring nearly 700 people in the bombing of a federal building in Oklahoma.

Ms. Janet Reno: Before she became the Attorney General for the U.S., she was State Attorney for Florida. She and I shared a platform where we gave speeches at the Fontainebleau Hotel on Miami Beach. (Ms. Reno, and her aged mother, walked the two mile parade in Liberty city (Miami, Florida) for many years.

Dr. Joyce Brothers: Dr. Brothers and I shared a platform while speaking at Cobbs County Community College near Atlanta, Georgia, where I presented a paper on How African Americans have influenced America's lifestyle. (That was my first paid public speaking engagement.)

Dr. Jocelyn Elders: I first met Dr. Elders when she was head of the Health Department in Arkansas and I took a group of international doctors to meet with her. When she was appointed Surgeon General of the U.S. by President Clinton, I made a personal call on her in her office in DC.

Carrie Meeks: Ms. Meeks was the first African American from Florida to be elected to Congress since Reconstruction. I met Congresswoman Meeks when she and I would often attend conferences together in Miami. I visited with her a few times in her office in D.C.

Kendrick Meeks: I campaigned for and with former Congressman Meeks when he was running for office. In 2006 I took a group of underprivileged youth on their first trip outside of Dade County to Washington, D.C. Representative Meeks hosted us for a breakfast in the Senate dining room.

William Ryan: Mr. Ryan was a Congressman from New York. I worked in his office as an assistant to his office manager. My primary job was to write the first draft for many of his public speaking engagements.

Sam Walton: I met Mr. Walton before he established Walmart. He had already developed the largest distribution system in the world. I took an industrialist from France to tour the impressive plant. The Walton family hosted us for dinner in their home. His four children were present, and Alice, his daughter, was in charge of barbecuing steaks for the dinner.

Robert L. Johnson: Mr. Johnson was the former owner of BET, which he sold for several billion dollars, making him the richest Black person in America. During the days of apartheid in South Africa, I was assigned to work mainly with South African officials for 10 years leading up to the dismantling of that cursed system. The purpose was to help that nation end that draconian system without bloodshed. Mr. Johnson helped in this endeavor. A racially diverse group of lawyers, including the dean of The University of Johannesburg Law School, and I, travelled to High Point, N.C, where Mr. Johnson hosted us for four days.

Archbishop Desmond Tutu of South Africa: I met Bishop Tutu when he and his family were visiting Atlanta for an international meeting. He had just been awarded the Nobel Peace Prize. I was their State Department host for lunch. I was with them for three days.

President Vladimir Putin: I met Putin when he was touring the United States and made a stop in Miami where a reception was given to welcome him. I was invited to the reception and was singled out to take a photo with the Russian. He was not yet president.

President Jimmy Carter: I first met Mr. Carter at the Carter Center in Atlanta when I took a small group of Nigerian politicians to meet with him. (We also had a meeting with Congressman **John Lewis** during that visit to Atlanta). A couple of years later, I worked side by side with Mr. Carter when he came to Miami to participate in working on a project sponsored by Habitat for Humanity in Liberty City.

President Bill Clinton: When the President visited Miami, I was appointed by Sister Jeanne, the President of Barry University, to represent the university at the Dade county luncheon given for Bill Clinton.

Queen Elizabeth: When the Queen visited Miami, three hundred people were selected to dine with her and her husband. Mildred and I were honored to be among the invitees.

This account is not written as a crass form of name-dropping or of self-aggrandizement. This is important because it is an actual part of the Raiford family history. Only after writing this abbreviated autobiography did I realize that this history is steeped in struggle, tenacity, courage, perseverance, and tremendous good fortune. Who would have thought that a black boy, growing up poor in the rural south during the Jim Crow (legal apartheid) era would become personally acquainted with such world-renowned people as Mrs. Eleanor Roosevelt, Archbishop Tutu, Maria Callas, James Baldwin, and Queen Elizabeth? Who would have thought that he would go from working in the bean fields of Florida to teaching in some of the most prestigious universities in the nation? Who would have predicted that he would travel from Zuber to Paris, to London, to Rome, to Tokyo, to Sidney, and Moscow? Why were so many people favorably disposed to him? Why were so many life-threatening circumstances and situations thwarted? Why was he invariably navigated out of harm's way? The truth is, I honestly do not have a definite answer to any of these questions. I only know that my life has been comprised of unusual events...a life steeped in serendipity.